THE
PMI-ACP℠
EXAM

HOW TO PASS ON YOUR FIRST TRY

WRITTEN BY

Andy Crowe
PMI-ACP℠, CSM
PMP, PgMP

1ST EDITION

Andy Crowe, PMI-ACP, CSM, PMP, PgMP

"PMI," "PMP," "PMBOK" and "PMI-ACP" are certification marks in the United States and other nations, registered to the Project Management Institute, Inc.

Velociteach is a Global Registered Education Provider with the Project Management Institute.

All inquiries should be addressed to (e-mail): *info@velociteach.com*

First Edition, First Printing: February, 2012
ISBN: 978-0-9827608-3-3

ATTENTION CORPORATIONS, UNIVERSITIES, COLLEGES, & PROFESSIONAL ORGANIZATIONS. Quantity discounts are available on bulk purchases of this book. For information, please contact *info@velociteach.com*.

Dedicated to the loving memory of Barbara Crowe.

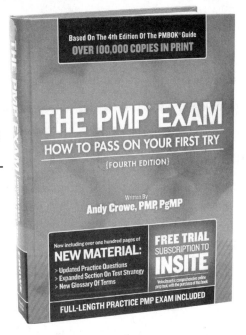

THE PMP EXAM
How to Pass on Your First Try

The most trusted book on the PMP exam with everything you need to prepare and pass conveniently organized in a single reference.

ALPHA PROJECT MANAGERS

Imagine having access to the top project managers from organizations and industries around the world and having the chance to uncover what they do, how they approach their challenges and what they know. This book gets you inside the minds of these top managers and shares their practices, their attitudes and their secrets.

My journey with Agile began in the late 1990s when I sat through a presentation on a new methodology known as the Rational Unified Process. I had stumbled into this through an interest in the Unified Modeling Language. During this presentation, the facilitator mentioned that he had been working with teams that worked with no actual project manager. He referred to this as "Agile." I peppered the instructor with questions and left with my head spinning.

Years later, I was developing the methodology for a corporation in Atlanta when a former colleague invited me to lunch. He had me come by his workplace downtown to meet the development team.

When I entered the room, I noticed there was something different. The team all sat around one oval table, and there were index cards all over the walls and tables. The team was finishing an estimating exercise where each member would write an estimate on one of these cards and then everyone would turn them over simultaneously and the haggling process would begin. To someone who had not practiced Agile, I didn't understand why multiple people had to estimate the same work. After all, I was taught that the most important estimate came from the person who would actually be doing the work. The team explained that they were practing something called "Scrum," and that they would all be collectively responsible for the project and for the results.

At this point, I was more than intrigued. Shortly after that, I had an opportunity to participate in my first Agile project. All of the development were both seasoned and senior. The project was high-profile, and the goal was to get working software into the customer's hands as quickly (and as frequently) as possible.

My first experience was amazing. The iterations went by in a blur, and the project was deployed and updated regularly. The customer, who was embedded on our team, was enthralled, and I quickly realized that I was learning more than I was contributing. It seemed like every day some new technique was introduced to our team.

From that point on, I would have a foot firmly in both the Agile and the traditional world.

This book represents an exciting milestone for me. I have written about project management for the main part of my career, but this is the first dedicated book on Agile I have undertaken. I can honestly say that I enjoyed every minute of it. I hope you can say the same after reading it!

Andy Crowe, PMI-ACP, CSM, PMP, PgMP

How To Use This Book

This book is not a book on how to practice Agile, although practitioners may well benefit from reading it. It is a book on how to pass the PMI-ACP exam, and those who are preparing to sit for the exam will find everything they need to know in this volume. There are many other wonderful books on Agile that practitioners will certainly want to consult.

The glossary is a very important part of this book. Read it and read it again. Knowing it well will help you answer questions on the actual PMI-ACP exam. It is recommended that you scan it once before reading the chapters and then again as you finish the book.

The chapters are written to balance technical accuracy with readability. Every attempt was made to help the reader understand.

The decision was made to capitalize the word "Agile" throughout the book. Many resources follow this, and many others do not. The main reason that tipped the scales was that the PMI-ACP exam capitalizes it throughout.

The words "Team", "Customer" and "Product Owner" and other roles are often capitalized. This is because the most popular methodology, Scrum, treats them as formal roles and capitalizes them, but it is not unusual to see this convention followed in other Agile resources.

In most cases, the attempt was made to be gender-inclusive; however, at times this makes the text awkward or difficult to understand. In those cases, masculine or feminine pronouns were often used.

There is a trial key to InSite in the back of this book. This will provide you with access to more sample PMI-ACP questions in an environment that simulates the exam. If you do not have a keycard, it is possible that your book is not legitimate. Contact the publisher for more information.

The questions in this book were designed to be very slightly more difficult than the actual PMI-ACP; however, they are also highly aligned with the content of this book. Scoring 80% or better on the final exams in this book is a good sign that you are ready to sit for the PMI-ACP exam. If you have taken these exams too many times to get a valid score, sign onto *http://insite.velociteach.com* to receive more sample questions in a simulated test environment.

About the Author

Andy Crowe is the world's best-selling project management author. In addition to this book, he has authored <u>The PMP Exam: How To Pass On Your First Try</u> and <u>Alpha Project Managers: What The Top 2% Know that Everyone Else Does Not</u>. Crowe is founder and CEO of Velociteach, a company passionate about the dissemination of best practices in project management, headquartered in Kennesaw, GA.

He spends much of his time writing in the Blue Ridge Mountains.

Stay Current

Get updates from Andy on Twitter at *twitter.com/andycrowe*

Ask exam-related questions, participate in discussions, and stay on top of trends and best practices in project management by communicating with Andy and the Velociteach team via their project management blog at *savvypm.velociteach.com*

Facebook

Get exam tips, ask questions, and access special offers by liking this book at *facebook.com/PMIACPExam*

About Velociteach

Velociteach, a Kennesaw, GA company, has experienced dramatic growth since its founding in 2002. This growth combined with Velociteach's commitment to excellent training and "outrageous customer service" have made it the industry leader in PMP certification preparation and project management training.

As a Global Registered Education Provider (R.E.P.) with the Project Management Institute, Velociteach offers training around the world, teaching certification and advanced project management theory and practice.

Velociteach offers live classroom, distance, and e-learning courses around the world. Full details on this and other course offerings are available online at *www.velociteach.com.*

Contents

Chapter 7– Working With Agile 101

Chapter 8– Coaching with Agile 119

Chapter 9– Agile Methodologies 137

CHAPTER ONE

UNDERSTANDING AGILE

We'll begin the thrust of this book by looking at the Agile philosophy and how Agile projects differ from the traditional way of managing projects. Exploring the similarities and differences between Agile and traditional project management will help you on the PMI-ACP exam: especially because the exam has traps set up to trick people who approach the exam oriented in a traditional mind set.

Things can change slowly in the world of project management. Mostly, it's a straightforward profession. Needs are defined and are translated into goals. The goals are translated into features and functionality. This, in turn, is broken down into tasks it would take to create the desired components. Progress is communicated, work is performed, and everything is tested and delivered to the customer. The beauty is that regardless of the methodology your project follows, the aforementioned steps have to be accomplished.

Given the previous sentence, you may wonder how different methodologies can be? After all, with so much in common, they must look more alike than different; however, in actual practice, methodologies can differ so greatly that they bear almost no resemblance. People who attempt to switch from one methodology to another often find it nearly impossible to make the transition. It can require not just a change in practice, but also a change in thinking.

METHODOLOGIES

Before we go any farther, it is important to understand what we mean by the word "methodology." A methodology is a set of processes and practices performed a specific way in order to accomplish a project. For example, an organization may have a specific methodology that prescribes a series of meetings with defined deliverables that need to be produced. These deliverables may follow a workflow to get approval. There may be checklists and policies that are followed, and all of this needs to be done for each project of this type. All of these would make up the organization's methodology.

Methodologies are incredibly important. An organization which has a mature, effective, and repeatable methodology has an advantage over competitors who do not have this level of process. Some consulting organizations prize their methodologies much the way top chefs treasure their recipes (and for many of the same reasons), and some even build entire marketing strategies around them.

Organizations with no methodology tend to rely on the heroic effort of their employees. Successes are not repeatable, and lessons from failures are not implemented back into future efforts.

Actually, a methodology can be thought of as being similar to a professional team's game strategy. It's a way of working within the rules to achieve results and goals, and it needs to provide focus for planning for an end result while being flexible and adaptable to the present situation.

When we talk about "Agile," we are essentially referring to a family of methodologies. You can make some assumptions about what an Agile project is like, but there are numerous Agile methodologies (this book covers Scrum, XP, and Lean), and sometimes how they differ is as striking as are the things they have in common.

TRADITIONAL WATERFALL PROJECTS

The focus of this book is the Agile approach, but before we go too far down that path, let's take a moment and discuss the traditional way. If you've never practiced traditional project management, this will help you to understand some of the reasons that Agile is the way it is.

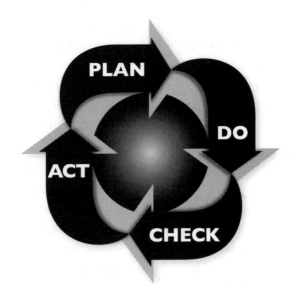

Since the end of World War II, project management has primarily followed a path that became known as the "waterfall" approach. It derived its name from the linear way in which activities flow from high level to low level. Waterfall, like Agile, really represents a whole family of methodologies that follow this approach.

Deming's Plan-Do-Check-Act Cycle

Much of waterfall came into being with the Deming Cycle of Plan-Do-Check-Act cycle. What may seem like common sense today was quite revolutionary at the time it was introduced.

Waterfall methodologies generally rely on a heavy up-front analysis and documentation of the need and problems, along with the proposed solution. A plan is formed, and then all or part of the solution is constructed, the results are compared with the plan, and corrective action is taken as necessary.

Perhaps no methodology illustrates the waterfall approach better than the Systems Development Life Cycle (SDLC).

SDLC is a robust methodology that breaks the life cycle down into phases, with the analysis, design, implementation, testing, and evaluation carried out in each phase. Specific activities and deliverables are prescribed for each phase.

The SDLC Waterfall

While traditional, waterfall, project management does have its strong points, practitioners began to notice that there are also corresponding weaknesses. Projects often become rigid and resistant to change, even if that change is good for the project. Others noted that waterfall projects can sometimes become more about the process than the product. Organizations that practice this for years can often become more interested in how something is done rather than why it is done or what the results are. Another criticism of waterfall projects is that they require so much up-front analysis that the team commits to technical solutions too early in the project, and many traditional projects kept the customers at bay, requiring them to sign off on a requirements document that they may not fully understand and wait months before they can put their hands on a product. By the time they see and touch a product, it may be what they asked for but far from what they wanted or needed.

THE AGILE WAY

When Agile project management came into being in the mid 1990s, it represented a true shift, both in thinking and in practice for project managers. Many argue that it was the first significant shift within project management in recent history.

This new approach changes quite a bit. Under the old way, management generally told everyone what to do. The manager was often euphemistically referred to as the "smartest guy in the room" (and the smartest person must also be the most senior person – right?).

That is not the Agile way. Agile turns that approach around. Rather than the smartest or most senior person dictating the work that is done, a team may conduct a dozen experiments to see which way works best. The theory is that one person may be smarter than the rest of us, but no one is smarter than all of us.

Teams are no longer organized hierarchically with direction coming from the top down. Instead, Agile projects value self-organizing teams with no formal project manager. This means that the work is distributed by team consensus rather than by an authority. After all, who is better to decide what to work on than the team who will be doing the work? The project makes decisions as a team with a continued focus on delivering value to the customer. Meetings and the project work itself are conducted out in the open, with communication flowing freely among all team members.

As work progresses, communication is out in the open. Daily stand-up meetings are held each morning so that each team member can communicate what they worked on yesterday, what is planned for today, and what obstacles they are encountering. Information radiators (covered later) are posted in highly visible locations and are kept updated to communicate the project's progress to everyone who sees them.

When problems arise, rather than escalating these to a manager, the team works to resolve them internally, and because of the high degree of visibility and transparency, it is difficult for team members to hide any poor performance.

Agile projects are welcoming to change, and when product or functional changes are introduced, the team embraces them. This is true even if the changes are introduced late in the project or if they affect the architecture. The team will meet, evaluate the change, and look at the impact and ways in which it can be incorporated into the project.

Customer involvement is a key part of any Agile methodology. This means that the customer participates in meetings and has complete visibility into the team's progress. He communicates priorities by focusing on the value a feature would provide and then balancing that against the amount of work it would take to implement the functionality. The customer is not punished or penalized when he changes his mind, rather, it is not only understood that priorities shift and change, but it is expected.

Work is delivered to the customer in small, frequent releases. This has numerous benefits. For one, it keeps the team's focus very sharp by giving it an immediate priority (to build a set of functionality into the next iteration). Another benefit is that it gets that functionality into the hands of the customer quickly, allowing it to be used, tested, and providing a rapid feedback loop. Still another benefit is that the team integrates various functions back into the overall system quickly, bringing any potential architecture or integration issues to the surface more rapidly (e.g., if one feature breaks or conflicts with another feature, this should be discovered relatively quickly).

If a question arises about which path to take, the Agile team may execute a "spike,f" or rapid experiment, to determine the best way to proceed.

When practicing Agile, a retrospective is held at the end of each iteration and each release. This provides time for the team to reflect and communicate what worked well in the previous cycle and what did not work. The point of this is not merely to discuss any issues, but to address them with the ultimate goal of continuous improvement (Kaizen).

All of this leads to an entirely new approach. Instead of the traditional way where a product is planned extensively and then executed and finally tested, the Agile way more closely follows the model of envisioning and then evolving and adapting.

You may notice here that one of the key differences is that while the traditional model favors anticipation, the Agile model favors adaptation.

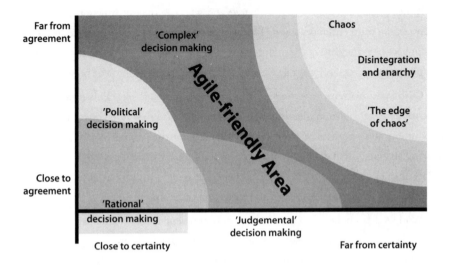

Stacey Diagram

This is a significant departure from the way things have been done. To contrast it, keep in mind that about half of the processes identified in The PMBOK Guide are considered to be planning processes, with many of these focused on producing relatively heavy documentation before executing the work packages.

Another key difference is that traditional methods of project management typically involved the customer early in the process but tended to keep the customer at arm's length once the project team began executing work packages. Agile projects are different. The customer is more closely involved at the time the work is being performed.

By this time, you may be thinking that the Agile approach sounds more like a "Ready. Fire. Aim!" approach, but that is not the case. Agile projects take small steps, getting the information in the hands of the customer as quickly as possible and evaluating not only the quality of the product but the quality of the overall process. Work is still planned, but the steps are much smaller, reducing the risk and the opportunity for mistakes.

So is Agile always the best choice for managing a project? Not necessarily. Agile works well in projects where there is a need for complex decision making. If a project already knows most of the details and things are close to agreement and close to certainty, then a waterfall methodology may be the best choice. The same argument can be made for a chaotic project environment, since a commanding and controlling style of leadership could bring order. The illustration, known as a Stacey Diagram, illustrates this spectrum of environments.

SUMMARY

There are many differences between Agile projects and traditional waterfall projects. They have notably different practices, the teams are organized differently, and team members who function well within one methodology may struggle under the other. As we will see further into this book, Agile projects also produce very different project communications and artifacts.

And yet, despite all of these differences, both waterfall and Agile projects are generally focused on the same goals of delivering a well-tested product that satisfies the customer within an efficient time frame that doesn't leave the team worn out (or worse) at the end.

Before we get into the specifics of Agile projects, how they are managed, and how they differ from traditional ones, let's take some time to look at the PMI-ACP exam itself and what you can expect as you prepare for it.

THE PMI-ACP EXAM

CHAPTER TWO

THE PMI-ACP EXAM

INTRODUCTION

This chapter will explain the PMI-ACP Certification Exam, what it is like, and the material it covers. It will explain exactly what the test is, how it is structured, and how to apply for it. Specific strategies on how to pass the exam will be discussed in Chapter 10 – How to Pass the PMI-ACP Exam.

BACKGROUND ON THE PMI-ACP EXAM

The Project Management Institute (PMI) was founded in 1969. Up until that point, most of the emphasis in management was put on functional management such as managing departments and people.

In 1984, PMI took a small group of project managers through the first Project Management Professional (PMP) credential process. The exam was based on accepted best practices within project management, and it quickly became known as an infamously difficult exam. Popularity soared over the years, and today there are over 400,000 PMPs worldwide.

It was not until 1987 when the first Guide to the Project Management Body of Knowledge, or PMBOK Guide, (pronounced "pimbock guide") was created. This was an attempt to organize the accepted best practices in one reference. The first PMBOK Guide was a relatively short white paper and bore only a passing resemblance to current editions, but it was an important step. The PMBOK Guide became an ANSI specification for project management and ended up on the shelf of countless project managers around the world.

But times change, and many in the information technology world found the planning-heavy PMBOK approach to be unwieldy and slow to adapt to change. Some practitioners were starting to experiment with a new way.

While thousands of project managers looked to PMI for guidance on how to apply Agile, it was often difficult to find. To put it in perspective, the word "Agile" did not even appear in the 1st, 2nd, 3rd, or 4th editions of the PMBOK Guide, which was the standard for managing individual projects. This topic was vigorously debated within the community. What was a project manager to do if he worked in an organization that embraced Agile but wanted to do things "the PMI way?" Could a PMP ethically uphold PMI's code of conduct while practicing Agile project management?

More practically, was there a way to reconcile Agile's adaptive and experiment-heavy approach with PMI's preference for more careful advanced planning?

Many project managers struggled with how these two systems could be reconciled on an actual project, if at all. Some argued that the more traditional approach outlined in previous PMBOK Guides was not compatible with Agile since it more closely followed a "command and control" model and relied heavily on knowing and planning prior to execution, while Agile rejected much of this, relying instead upon self-organization, smaller experiments and adaptation.

But others argued that the systems could be reconciled. After all, every project had to be planned to some degree or another, and the overall cycle of planning, execution, and monitoring and control still held. Whether a team followed a traditional waterfall approach or an Agile approach for their project, the truth of the matter was that many of the same steps were still performed, even if the process looked different, the teams emphasized different activities, and many of the outputs likely looked different. Also, the PMBOK Guide did include some Agile-like tools and techniques, such as progressive elaboration and rolling wave planning.

The two groups were poised to come closer together, and in 2010 PMI formalized the effort by moving forward with an effort to reconcile Agile with the PMBOK Guide and create a new certification in the process. This turned out to be no small effort. Decisions had to be made about whether or not a separate standard would be created and how this would be reflected in the 5th Edition PMBOK Guide.

In 2011, PMI launched the pilot program for the PMI-ACP certification. Over the next few months, a pilot group was taken through the application process and sat for the exam. The pilot ended in November of 2011, and in January of 2012 the process was opened up to anyone who wanted to apply.

WHAT THE EXAM TESTS

Before we discuss what the PMI-ACP Certification Exam does test, let's clear up a few misconceptions about the exam.

THE PMI-ACP CERTIFICATION EXAM DOES NOT TEST:

- Your Agile management experience
- Your common sense
- Your knowledge of industry practices
- Your knowledge of how to use software tools
- What you learned in management school
- How good an Agile practitioner you are
- Your intelligence

THE PMI-ACP CERTIFICATION EXAM DOES TEST:

- Your knowledge of Agile practices
- Your understanding of the many terms that are used to describe Agile
- Your ability to apply established Agile practices in a variety of hypothetical situations
- Your understanding of certain Agile methodologies
- Your understanding of PMI's testing biases

A PASSING GRADE

When the first few hundred people took the PMI-ACP exam in the second half of 2011, their results were withheld for a few months, evaluated in a large batch, and graded on a curve. Most who took the exam during that time did not find out whether they passed or failed for several months. This was to establish a passing baseline for the exam, and like many exams it was designed so that a certain percentage of people would fail.

The exam is pass/fail, and while PMI keeps the passing threshold a secret, research indicates that the passing percentage is somewhere around 69%.

Some people find it very difficult to understand why they cannot study and make a perfect score on the PMI-ACP. It is a good thing to want to do well on the exam, but considering the breadth of material, simply passing it is a terrific accomplishment! Agile experts debate some of the questions, and there will be some that you will be absolutely certain you got right that you likely missed.

Your goal in taking the PMI-ACP should be to do your absolute best and to make sure that your best effort falls within PMI's passing score limits.

THE EXAM MATERIAL

When you sit for the PMI-ACP Exam, you will be required to answer exactly 120 questions, *but only 100 of those questions will count toward your passing score.* The other 20 questions are experimental questions that PMI is evaluating for use on future exams. The good news is that these 20 questions do not count toward your grade. The bad news is that you will never know which questions count and which do not, as they are sprinkled throughout.

PMI provides some information about the exam in their published Exam Content Outline document published here:

www.pmi.org/~/media/Files/PDF/Agile/PMI_Agile_Certification_Content_Outline.ashx

(Be aware that, many people who have prepared for the exam reported that they did not consider this document to be overly useful).

GETTING TO THE TEST
(THE APPLICATION)

It is recommended that you join the Project Management Institute prior to signing up to take the test. As of April 1, 2012, the new member fee is $139.00 ($129.00 membership + $10.00 new member activation fee). Application may be made online at *www.pmi.org*, or you may obtain an application from PMI by calling (610) 356-4600.

After joining PMI, you will receive a membership number that you can use to receive a $60.00 discount on the exam's non-member fee. The Examination Fee will be $435.00 for a member in good standing. If you elect not to join PMI, it will cost $495.00 to apply to take the test (note that the aforementioned prices are based on computer-based testing prices. If you are taking the paper test through an authorized proctor, the cost will be $50.00 less).

In addition to the savings, there are many other benefits that come with joining PMI, including a subscription to PMI's publications, PM Network and PM Today; discounts on books and PMI-sponsored events; and access to a wealth of information in the field of project management.

When you get ready to apply for eligibility for PMI-ACP Certification, you can apply online or use printed forms (also available online). If at all possible, you should apply online. Wait times may change, depending on the time of year and the demand, but applicants typically report turnaround times from one to two weeks. The length of time can vary, depending on the volume of applications that PMI is processing. In any case, you must have your letter of eligibility from PMI before you can sit for the PMI-ACP Certification Exam.

To be eligible for PMI-ACP Certification, you will need to demonstrate that you meet the minimum criteria. The current qualifications that PMI requires are summarized in the following list of requirements.

REQUIREMENTS TO APPLY

-   Secondary degree (high school diploma, associates degree, or global equivalent)

-   2,000 hours of project management experience accumulated over the previous five years

-   1,500 hours of Agile-specific experience accumulated over the previous two years

-   21 hours of project management education (http://InSite.velociteach.com has many affordable options for online e-learning if you need training or "contact hours").

ONGOING EDUCATION

PMI-ACPs are expected to demonstrate not only knowledge and experience but also their ongoing commitment to the field of project management. To promote such commitment, PMI requires that all PMI-ACPs maintain their certification status by completing at least 30 Professional Development Units (PDUs) every 36 months. The requirements for PDUs are defined in further detail in the PMI Continuing Certification Requirements Program Handbook given to all PMI-ACPs, and these requirements are similar in nature to requirements that legal, medical, and other professions have adopted.

THE TESTING ENVIRONMENT

The PMI-ACP Certification Exam is administered in a formal environment. There is no talking during the exam, and you cannot bring notes, books, paper, cell phones, PDAs, or calculators into the examination room with you. The PMI-ACP is very carefully monitored, and test-takers are observed by the test proctor and are under recorded video and audio surveillance. This can be distracting as well as unnerving, so it is important to be mentally prepared as you walk into the exam.

Most people take the exam on a computer. This test is delivered on a standard Windows-based PC that runs a secure, proprietary testing application. The computer setup is very straightforward, with a mouse and keyboard and a simple graphical user interface used to display the test. PMI can arrange special accommodations for those test-takers who have special physical needs.

Recently, PMI has also made provisions for test-takers to receive the test in paper form. While this book references the computerized version of the exam, the content on both versions of the exam is identical, and your preparation should not be any different. More information on the paper-based testing (PBT) may be found online at *www.pmi.org*.

The exam ends either when your three-hour time limit has been reached (more on this in a moment) or when you choose to end the exam. Once the exam is over, you will know your score within a few seconds, and those results are electronically transmitted to PMI. If you passed, you are immediately a "PMI-ACP," and you may start using that designation after your name. PMI will mail you all of the official information within a few weeks. If you did not pass, you may schedule to take the exam again. You may take it up to three times in a calendar year. If you do not pass on your third attempt, you must wait one year from your last attempt to reapply.

TIME LIMIT

Taking a test while the clock is ticking can be unnerving. The PMI-ACP is a long exam, but you are given a significant block of time to complete the test. From the time you begin the exam, you will have 180 minutes (3 hours) to finish. For most people, this is enough time to take the test and review the answers. The allocation works out to 90 seconds per question if no breaks are taken. While a few of the more complicated questions will certainly require more than 90 seconds, most will take much less time. This is even more true given the fact that the great majority of questions are relatively short and straightforward.

The subject of time management for the exam, along with a suggested strategy for managing your time, is covered later in Chapter 10 - How to Pass the PMI-ACP Exam.

QUESTION FORMAT

Exam questions are given in a multiple choice format, with four possible answers, marked A, B, C, and D, and only one of those four answers is correct. Unlike in some exams, there is no penalty for guessing, so it is to your advantage to answer every question on the PMI-ACP exam, leaving none of them blank.

If you are familiar with other PMI exams, you will be glad to know that the questions are generally quite a bit shorter and more direct on the PMI-ACP exam. This elimination of testing "noise" is likely due to the increased role of Professional Examination Service in the development of the exam. Going through all the sample questions provided in this volume is an excellent way to prepare for the types of questions you will encounter on the actual exam.

If you have taken the PMP Exam, you know that the questions can be difficult to understand. Given comparable levels of knowledge, the PMI-ACP Exam should be slightly easier than the PMP Exam due to the wording of the questions and answers.

SUMMARY

Passing the PMI-ACP Exam is no small feat; however, by focusing on the materials in this book, you should find it to be straightforward. The amount of time per question that you have on this exam will work in your favor more than on other PMI certification exams. The key for this exam is to focus on learning the material and the test biases and not worrying so much about tricky wording on questions. Focusing your study on the next few chapters will pay big dividends.

CHAPTER THREE

AGILE MANIFESTO & PRINCIPLES

INTRODUCTION

The Manifesto For Agile Software Development is an important part of the PMI-ACP exam, but the good news is that this is one of the easier sections of the exam. You will need to have a general understanding of the Manifesto and a solid knowledge of the value sets it contains. You should expect to see several questions on the exam directly related to this material.

HISTORY

The drafting of the Manifesto For Agile Software Development represents a milestone in Agile's history. Numerous Agile methodologies had become popular in the mid-1990s, and in 2001, a group of 17 of their advocates came together in Snowbird, Utah and drafted the document that would set out the organizing principles for Agile. Essentially, this was what the different Agile methodologies had in common.

When you read the Manifesto, you will notice that it is high-level. This is because Agile methodologies agree on the big picture, but the specifics will differ from one methodology to another. For example, all Agile methodologies will support the concept of "Individuals and interactions over processes and tools," but these interactions will likely look very different when looking at a Scrum project and an XP project (two of the Agile methodologies covered in Chapter 9), and the processes and tools will probably vary even more.

The Agile Manifesto emphasizes what these methodologies all have in common under the Agile umbrella.

THE AGILE MANIFESTO
MANIFESTO FOR AGILE SOFTWARE DEVELOPMENT

*We are uncovering better ways of developing software by doing it
and helping others do it. Through this work we have come to value:*

- Individuals and interactions *over processes and tools*

- Working software *over comprehensive documentation*

- Customer collaboration *over contract negotiation*

- Responding to change *over following a plan*

*That is, while there is value in the items on the right,
we value the items on the left more*

Kent Beck	*James Grenning*	*Robert C. Martin*
Mike Beedle	*Jim Highsmith*	*Steve Mellor*
Arie van Bennekum	*Andrew Hunt*	*Ken Schwaber*
Alistair Cockburn	*Ron Jeffries*	*Jeff Sutherland*
Ward Cunningham	*Jon Kern*	*Dave Thomas*
Martin Fowler	*Brian Marick*	

HOW THE MANIFESTO IS USED

The Manifesto For Agile Software Development (sometimes referred to as the Agile Manifesto) is important in actual practice. It represents guiding principles. It is expected that Agile practitioners are going to disagree on many implementation details, but if they are implementing something that conflicts with the Agile Manifesto, then there is a problem. The good news is that the document is broad enough to include many different methods and practices and specific enough to give helpful guidance to component methodologies.

In other words, if it ever comes down to a tiebreaker, the Agile Manifesto wins.

AGILE MANIFESTO VALUES

For the PMI-ACP Exam, you will want to understand the four paired core values (you do not need to know the names of the ones who signed the document). Each pair is presented as something that is valued more than something else.

You should expect to see these values on the exam, so learn them carefully.

Let's take a look at each of the four pairs.

1. Individuals and interactions over processes and tools

Projects are accomplished through people. Processes and tools may help people, but they do not get work done.

This first value pair is no small statement. Anyone who has ever worked for a large, mature organization may have found themselves doing something and wondering why. (One software developer who was in the military told this author of a time when he was required to paint a building that was slated for demolition in nine days simply because regulations called for it to be painted).

While processes and tools may be a good thing, they can also get in the way.

By this time, you're probably coming to the conclusion that Agile is a fairly irreverent family of methodologies, and you would be right. This is particularly true with Lean (covered in Chapter 9), which constantly evaluates and ruthlessly disregards anything that does not add value. Agile is ultimately pragmatic. It trades convention for what works, and when processes and tools are part of that convention, they may be left out.

Agile projects put a very heavy emphasis on teamwork, and one of the ways in which teamwork is manifested through the shared ownership of the code. Agile teams believe that all of the code is collectively owned by the team and not just by the person who wrote it.

But the idea of individuals and interactions goes beyond the previous example or even the paired programming practices of XP (also covered in Chapter 9). It is the very fabric of Agile projects. Tools and processes may or may not add value, but without a strong team and healthy interactions, Agile methodologies do not work.

2. Working software over comprehensive documentation

This is a very welcome value to most teams since it is a fact that most software developers do not relish writing documentation. Ideally, most programmers like to believe they can write self-documenting code.

The value of working software is important, because this supports the goal. After all, it is working software (not documentation) that delivers high value to the customer and the users. In general, progress on an Agile project is tracked and reported by how much working software is developed over time. A document expresses what is intended, but as the saying goes, "nothing speaks louder than code."

But that is not the end of the story. Some documentation is beneficial and necessary on the vast majority of projects. Teams change, and memory is lost. Agile wrestles with this by seeking to provide just enough documentation. This is what Agile pioneer, Alistair Cockburn, refers to as "barely sufficient documentation." The rule that drives this is that any documentation that is created should be tied directly to the value it creates for the customer, whether now or in the future.

3. Customer collaboration over contract negotiation

The point of this pair is that the closer you are to your customer, the better. The customer is the best person to specify what he or she wants, even when that process involves some trial and error. Trying to force all of that to occur in the contract phase is not only unrealistic - it's unproductive.

Orientation is important too. Would you prefer to be pitted against your customers across the negotiation table, haggling out a contract and punishing them for each change or working with your customer on a solution that benefits everyone?

Agile has you and your customer on the same side of the table. That does not mean that there won't be a contract. It does mean that Agile teams prefer to expend energy pulling in the same direction as the customer rather than to expend that energy opposing the customer.

4. Responding to change over following a plan

Agile was originally created to be applied to software projects, and anyone who has worked on a software project knows that it is the nature of these projects to change. Even the underlying technology is changing at such a rapid rate (e.g., Moore's Law and the regular introduction of new devices) that new avenues and possibilities are constantly being opened.

But technology projects have been managed with the same methodologies that were designed for construction projects and aircraft. While these top-down methodologies can work for technology projects, they do not always handle change particularly well. Instead, there can be great momentum toward sticking to the original plan where possible.

This makes sense, for instance, on the construction project for a new office building. Everything from the civil engineering to the architecture to the procurement of materials has to be done with a good understanding of how the end result will look, so change is discouraged on such a project. One construction firm had a noted strategy for underbidding projects at a loss only to make their profit on the ensuing, highly profitable change orders.

AGILE PRINCIPLES

In addition to the Agile Manifesto, there is a supporting document of 12 principles that provides a bit more detail and helps flesh out some of these concepts. These are presented below. In many cases on the PMI-ACP exam, you will have narrowed things down to two potential correct answers, and understanding these principles should help you get to the right answer.

Principles behind the Agile Manifesto
We follow these principles:

PRINCIPLE ONE

Our highest priority is to satisfy the customer through early and continuous delivery of valuable software.

The three words to home in on here are "early," "continuous," and "valuable". Expect to see these concepts repeatedly on the exam. Agile teams get working software into the customer's hands quickly and update it often, and this is prioritized by the value it brings the customer.

PRINCIPLE TWO
Welcome changing requirements, even late in development. Agile processes harness change for the customer's competitive advantage.

This represents a very significant departure from traditional waterfall project management, which views changing requirements with unease. In fact, one of the tenets of traditional project management is to seek to influence the factors that cause change.

Agile views this differently. It expects that requirements will change and actually welcomes those changes, even if they occur late in the project. Responding quickly to change and adapting to it can give the customer a significant competitive advantage to emerging opportunities.

This can be a hard value for traditional practitioners to embrace, but it is a very important concept to embrace for the exam.

PRINCIPLE THREE
Deliver working software frequently, from a couple of weeks to a couple of months, with a preference to the shorter time scale.

Different Agile methodologies specify different iteration cycles, but all of them are relatively short. The point is to get a working product in the hands of the customer quickly and to use that product to get meaningful feedback. Some methodologies, such as Scrum, have iterations specified at around one month, while more rigorous ones like XP focus on very rapid, one week iterations.

Short iterations provide structure for the team and enforce a continual disciplined focus on customer value.

PRINCIPLE FOUR
Business people and developers must work together daily throughout the project.

There was a time when projects strictly segregated the ones responsible for the business value and the software developers. The thinking was that each group could focus on what they did best and business analysts and project leads could bridge the gap.

Agile projects do away with this model by bringing the customer and developers together, often having them work in the same physical space. This way there is no gap between the developers and the business people. This makes sense because in reality they share a common goal of working software that delivers value to the customer.

PRINCIPLE FIVE
Build projects around motivated individuals. Give them the environment and support they need, and trust them to get the job done.

While this may sound like common sense, traditional project management earned a reputation for often micromanaging employees, telling them how to do something and not just what to do. This is an often-unintended consequence of top-down management.

Agile projects build a solid team and actively avoid micromanaging. That is not to say that a developer will not ever be told how to do something, but this should come organically from a self-organizing team and not from a top-down edict.

PRINCIPLE SIX
The most efficient and effective method of conveying information to and within a development team is face-to-face conversation.

Informal oral communication is much more popular on Agile projects than formal written communication is. The idea is that two people sitting down together and working on a solution are more effective than if they are emailing back and forth or exchanging paper.

Face-to-face communication is the backbone of Agile projects. Unlike traditional projects where a significant amount of communication may take place in breakout meetings, on Agile projects communication takes place in the open, and the entire team generally has access to all conversations.

The term "osmotic communication" describes the effect of how team members pick up information just by being in the same room or general area where a conversation is taking place.

PRINCIPLE SEVEN
Working software is the primary measure of progress.

Plans and documents may be useful, but when the underlying goals change they may lose much of their value. Projects can become so obsessed with keeping documentation up to date that the documents become a liability.

Real value is conveyed through results, and results are expressed through software that works.

PRINCIPLE EIGHT
Agile processes promote sustainable development. The sponsors, developers, and users should be able to maintain a constant pace indefinitely.

In this case, sustainable development is focused on the team. While many projects have a big push at the end where the team works late hours and weekends, Agile projects do things differently. It is very likely that your Agile project will have a greater intensity than other projects (particularly with a methodology like XP), but they attempt to keep a steady, sustainable pace of work so that there are not intense pushes at the end of iterations and cycles.

The ideal goal is to keep a pace that can be sustained indefinitely so that team members do not experience burnout or exhaustion and perform at an optimal level for an indefinite period of time.

PRINCIPLE NINE
Continuous attention to technical excellence and good design enhances agility.

This principle does not need much explanation. The better the design, the easier it will be to maintain, and even change. More consistent and better quality will allow the team to respond to change more rapidly than a shoddy project will.

PRINCIPLE TEN
Simplicity—the art of maximizing the amount of work not done—is essential.

This principle is one embraced by all Agile methodologies, but particularly by Lean. The key is to maintain a consistent focus on customer value and to be ruthless about cutting activities that do not add value.

Keeping things simple is more than an aspiration; it is considered to be essential.

PRINCIPLE ELEVEN
The best architectures, requirements, and designs emerge from self-organizing teams.

Self-organization is one of the core components of an Agile team (this is discussed more in Chapter 5). When a team is self-organizing, it means that the team decides how work is allocated and who will work on a particular component and not the human resource department or management.

This is one of the most significant areas of difference between traditional and Agile projects, and not only are the teams self-organizing, but largely cross-functional as well.

PRINCIPLE TWELVE
At regular intervals, the team reflects on how to become more effective, then tunes and adjusts its behavior accordingly.

The one thing that is predictable on Agile projects is change. With traditional projects it is common to have meetings to reflect once the project or phase is completed; however, Agile tries to accomplish this more frequently through retrospectives. In an Agile retrospective, the team looks at the work that was accomplished in the last iteration or release and evaluates how to improve their practice the next time.

Daily stand-up meetings, where the team meets for 15 minutes each day, are another important way that team efforts are coordinated, and the team assesses and self-tunes. These are discussed in numerous places throughout this book.

The Declaration of Interdependence
for Modern Management

This declaration of interdependence was written by a group led by Alistair Cockburn and Jim Highsmith in 2005. It is intended to help philosophically guide Agile development, and although this document is not a formal exam reference, understanding it will help you on the PMI-ACP exam.

This declaration is made up of six statements. Do not focus your energy on memorization. Instead, make sure you understand the concepts and the philosophy they represent.

- *We increase return on investment*
  by making continuous flow of value our focus.

- *We deliver reliable results by engaging*
  customers in frequent interactions and shared ownership.

- *We expect uncertainty and manage for*
  it through iterations, anticipation and adaptation.

- *We unleash creativity and innovation by recognizing*
  that individuals are the ultimate source of value, and creating
  an environment where they can make a difference.

- *We boost performance through group accountability*
  for results and shared responsibility for team effectiveness.

- *We improve effectiveness and reliability through*
  situationally specific strategies, processes and practices.

SUMMARY

The Manifesto For Agile Software Development, the Principles Behind the Agile Manifesto, and The Declaration of Interdependence for Modern Management lay the philosophical groundwork for all Agile methodologies and for the PMI-ACP exam. By knowing the contents of these documents well, you will be able to answer several questions correctly and narrow down the choices on many others.

CHAPTER FOUR

PROJECT JUSTIFICATION

INTRODUCTION

Whether something is being performed in an Agile shop or in a more traditional environment, projects are often initiated in similar ways. Someone with the authority to spend money makes a decision to start a project, and that decision is based upon one or more criterion.

The material in this chapter is not Agile-specific, but it does apply to Agile projects.

PROJECT JUSTIFICATION

VALUE-BASED PRIORITIZATION

The idea behind value-based prioritization is that the project's value to the customer or market is given a financial number and is evaluated against other projects or opportunities. This is important, regardless of how the project will be managed. It is a rational way to determine which projects make the most sense.

PRESENT VALUE (PV) & NET PRESENT VALUE (NPV)

Present Value (PV) is based on the "time value of money" economic theory that a dollar today is worth more than a dollar tomorrow. If a project is expected to produce 3 annual payments of $100,000, then the present value (how much those payments are worth right now) is going to be less than $300,000. The reason for this is that you will not get your entire $300,000 until the 3rd year, but if you took $300,000 cash and put it in the bank right now or invest elsewhere, you would end up with more than $300,000 in 3 years.

PV is a way to take time out of the equation and evaluate how much a project is worth right now. It is important to understand that with PV, a bigger value is better.

Net Present Value (NPV) is the same as Present Value except that you also factor in your costs. For example, you have constructed a building with a PV of $500,000, but it cost you $350,000. In this case, your NPV would be $500,000 - $350,000 = $150,000.

The important points to remember for the exam are that a bigger PV or NPV makes a project more attractive, and that NPV calculations have already factored in the cost of the project.

INTERNAL RATE OF RETURN (IRR)

IRR, or "Internal Rate of Return," is a finance term used to express a project's returns as an interest rate. In other words, if the value of this project were an interest rate, what would it be? You should understand that just like the interest rate on a savings account, bigger is better when looking at IRR.

RETURN ON INVESTMENT (ROI)

Return On Investment is a percentage that shows what return you make by investing in something. Suppose, for example, that a company invests in a project that costs $200,000. The benefits of doing the project save the company $230,000 in the first year alone. In this case, the ROI would be calculated as the (benefit − cost) ÷ cost, or $30,000 ÷ $200,000 = 15%. For ROI, it is also important to keep in mind that bigger is better. If you were comparing a project with an ROI of 75% to one of a similar size with an ROI of 140%, the project with the ROI of 140% would be more desirable, all other things being equal.

COMPLIANCE

Compliance has become a very important topic over the past few years as government regulation of business has increased. In the United States, this took on particular urgency when the health-care HIPPA act was passed in 1996 and increased with the business and financial reporting-related Sarbanes-Oxley act in 2002. The Dodd-Frank Financial Act of 2010 brought this into the financial markets. Regulation has been on the sharp increase in recent years, and government agencies, businesses, and non-profits are required to be in compliance with these.

When considering compliance, it is important to understand that it is not optional. Compliance is required, even when there are other opportunities that may make money or have a higher return. Generally, when you see a project on the exam that is related to compliance with some regulation, you should highly favor it.

CHARTERING

Chartering is the act of pulling together an important document called the charter.

Throughout this book, it is stressed that Agile projects do not typically produce or value a lot of documentation, so you may be tempted to think that the charter is not very important for an Agile team. That would be incorrect. The charter is an exception to that rule, as it is both necessary and highly important. The good news is that it is usually only a page or two in length and can usually be produced fairly quickly.

A charter is used in both traditional waterfall projects and in Agile projects. It is the document that formally starts the project, names the project manager, and gives him or her the authority to apply resources to accomplish the project's goals.

Once an organization has selected a project or a contract is signed to perform a project, the project charter must be created. Following are the key facts you should know about the project charter.

THE PROJECT CHARTER

- The charter should be written as part of Iteration Zero
  if it does not already exist.

- It is created before actual project work commences.

- It is created based on some need, and it should explain that need.

- It is signed by the performing organization's senior management.

- It names the project manager and gives the PM authority
  to apply resources.

- It should include the high-level project requirements
  or critical success factors.

- It should include a high-level milestone view of the project schedule.

- It is a high-level document that does not include project details.

- It includes a summary-level preliminary project budget.

Watch out for any questions on the PMI-ACP exam that encourage you to skip the charter in favor of doing other work on the project or that lessen the importance of the charter.

SUMMARY

Agile projects are born largely in the same way as traditional projects. They require business justification and a charter. This part of the process is very similar to the way traditional projects are managed, but those roads are about to diverge sharply as you will see in subsequent chapters.

CHAPTER FIVE

TEAMS & TEAM SPACE

INTRODUCTION

The way in which teams function on Agile projects represents one of the most significant differences from traditional project management. This section explores how teams are organized, what kind of environment works best for them, and how they make decisions and carry out their work.

Be aware that the topic of "team" is a favorite area for the exam to try and trick test-takers by encouraging them to do things the traditional way.

SELF-ORGANIZATION OF TEAMS

You will see the term "self-organizing" used quite a lot in this book, and in any book on Agile project management. It is foundational to the concept and practice of Agile, and it requires quite a bit of change both in theory and in practice.

Traditional project management has settled into a top-down approach to organization. This was true from the earliest days of the industrial revolution where managers and engineers designed workflows and then plugged workers into repetitive tasks. The workers rarely got much input into the work they did or details about their environment. They were handed a job and expected to perform it, usually repetitively.

Over time, this evolved into a system where business analysts and project managers analyzed a problem, designed a solution, and divided the work into activities, which were estimated and then assigned to workers.

The flaws in this system are both numerous and apparent. First of all, if there is a weak link in the chain, the system fails. What if the business analyst did not properly understand the requirements? What if the estimates are seriously incorrect? Worse yet, what if the customer did not properly anticipate the underlying need or problem and imperfectly articulated a solution?

All of this began to change with the advent of Japanese Management after World War II. With help from Deming and others, the Japanese began to look at workflow differently. Workers began to have more input into how something was done. After all, who knew more about a task than the person doing the work? Workers were given quite a bit of input into how they did their jobs, how they organized their work, and even the production workflow. Nowhere was this truer than at the Japanese auto manufacturers, and within a few decades, they led the world in best practices and in quality.

Self-organization is nothing new. Examples in nature are abundant, such as birds and fish naturally organizing into flocks and schools, and natural occurrences of distributions as represented in Boyle's Law. Groups of people can and will self-organize in most situations.

This practice of listening to the worker began to find its way onto projects years later in some interesting ways. In the mid 1990s, methodologies began to spread that did away with much of the traditional top-down, planning-centric approach and instead handed a problem to a team and let them figure out how to solve it. These approaches favored letting the team (with participation from the customer) determine both what to do and how to go about doing it.

For the PMI-ACP Exam, know that self-organization is central to an Agile project. This process should be aided by the Coach or the ScrumMaster, but these roles must move from directing and controlling the team to coaching and facilitating.

At the same time, know that self-organization may not be able to resolve all team dysfunction. That is another big reason the role of Coach or ScrumMaster exists. For example, if the team has a culture that does not encourage conflict, this can be detrimental to the project. Conflict and the ability to resolve it the right way for the right reasons is a necessary attribute of a high-performing team. In fact, the right amount of conflict is as necessary to a project team as the resistance of water is to a speedboat motor. A skilled Coach might actually ask questions designed to introduce some conflict into the team in order to help the team (re)learn this skill. Obviously this needs to be done with great care.

Self-organizing goes beyond the initial team organization and allocation of work. It extends to self-managing and self-correcting, and it requires mature team members who can compromise, resolve conflict, and work toward a common goal. It extends to every part of how the project will be managed, including communications, team meetings, reporting, testing, bringing on new team members, and how to determine when work is "done."

But self-organization is only the means to an end. There is no direct benefit to the team organizing itself, but benefits do come as a result of this. For instance, as a result of being self-organizing, teams can more easily fulfill the goal of collective ownership of the code where no one individual has responsibility for a section of code or product, but instead all team members are collectively responsible for everything. Additionally, teams find it easier to communicate when they do not function as specialists, each controlling their own domain.

The main point of self-organization is that it provides a way for the team to succeed, fail, adjust, and improve together.

OPTIMAL TEAM SIZE

What is the right size for an Agile team? In his book <u>Succeeding with Agile</u>, author Mike Cohn suggests that if you cannot feed the team with "a couple of pizzas" then it is too large. This raises the obvious question "can Agile be applied to large projects?" The answer is "yes," but the project (and the team) needs to be divided. The general thought is that Agile does not scale well to large teams. Communication becomes chaotic, and self-organization breaks down (if it ever forms). The project has to be broken up into sub-projects, and the team has to be divided right along with it.

For Scrum (a specific Agile methodology covered in Chapter 9), co-creators Schwaber and Sutherland write in <u>The Scrum Guide</u> that the team size should be 7 ± 2. Some may deviate from this in actual practice, but it will give you a good frame of reference for the exam.

COLOCATION

Many projects, whether traditional or Agile, have seen benefits from colocating the team. This means different things on different projects, but Agile has some high aspirations for colocation.

At its most basic, colocating the team is the process of bringing all of the team members together in one place, but like many other things, Agile takes a cue from Nigel Tufnel and dials this up to 11.

Ideally configured Agile space not only has everyone in a single room, but also removes any barriers in the room. Team members, often including the customer, are placed around a square or circular table, facing each other. If they must exist, walls or partitions are kept very low, allowing people to freely see, hear, and interact with each other.

All of this increases the sense of a single, cohesive team, and the possibility of increased distractions should be more than offset by the richer flow of communication.

One of the issues traditional approaches have struggled with is the formation of silos on a project. Because traditional projects have organized people by specialty for a variety of reasons, individuals or team factions often work in isolation, focusing only on their area of expertise. Communication is often highly challenging across all of the different groups (which may, in turn, develop agendas of their own). The task of integrating all of these silos and the results of their work often falls to the project manager or some other group. Another problem this causes is when an isolated specialist leaves the project, significant knowledge is likely lost as well.

Colocation is just one of the ways in which Agile practitioners seek to do away with silos. Teams are not segregated by specialty, but everyone is put into the same space. Responsibility extends beyond an individual or pair's work product. Instead, the team shares collective responsibility for the entire product.

Because communication, cooperation, and a sense of team are so important for Agile projects to perform at their peak, attention should be paid to how that space is configured and outfitted. Communication is vital on Agile projects, and having all of the people who are on the project in a single space is a good place to start, but it is important that only people who actually contribute to the project are in the room.

The furniture should have no walls and should be oriented to allow people to talk to each other. Putting each programmer in a cube, facing away from the rest of the team, would nullify many of the benefits of collaborative space.

Another good idea is to work to encourage the team's ability to focus. Sometimes this means turning off notifications on computers (particularly pop-ups and audible alarms). Distractions can be very detrimental on a project, and repeated distractions can completely derail a team from getting any meaningful work done. Team members should be discouraged from using headphones or anything that might isolate them from the rest of the group.

Another important element is wall space that can help with collaboration. Having room to post useful information such as feature lists, backlogs and task lists, user stories, schedules, and the like will help the team get information at a glance. Highly visible information radiators are valuable tools to communicate inside to the team and outside to stakeholders. Most Agile teams also find it necessary to have plenty of whiteboard space in their war room.

These ideas for team space are by no means exhaustive. They are simply a place to begin. The important thing is to be deliberate and thoughtful so that the space supports the goals of communication and collaboration while allowing the team to focus and minimize distractions.

For the exam, consider colocation to be a highly desirable technique. If physical colocation is impossible, (for example, if the team is geographically distributed or virtual), then investing in software that simulates a live presence or lowers barriers would be a good idea. Whether it is software, processes, or some other practice, anything practitioners of Agile can do to facilitate collaborating and discourage team members from becoming siloed would be a step in the right direction.

TEAM SELECTION

Agile teams work best when they are made up of seasoned, skilled, and highly self-directed people. Unfortunately, these are also a scarce resource. The individuals you recruit to the project will have the largest impact on overall motivation.

To create a sustainable, motivated team, it is best to recruit people who are willing to work as part of a team, and preferably those who have successfully contributed in an Agile environment in the past. Since transparency and openness are so important on Agile projects, it is also important that the members understand that their work will be out in the open and that partitions (real or virtual) are not favored.

As team members are added, the existing team should be involved in interviewing and selecting new members.

TEAM PARTICIPATION

Agile teams are typically relatively small, with each member expected to make a positive, measurable contribution to the overall success of the project. The key to team participation is that each team member's contribution is visible to the entire team. The entire team motivation should rise as long as each member is contributing to project success at an acceptable rate.

ORGANIZATIONAL SUPPORT

Support is generally thought of as coming from outside the project, although it can also be from within, and it can have a tremendous impact on team motivation. Support is created when the right people are involved early in the project.

The customer or product owner is another source of support. Having a customer who not only believes in the project but also in the Agile process can be invaluable.

AGILE TOOLING

One of the biggest challenges Agile projects face is creating a solid team. Agile teams perform at their peak when the members participate together, ideally in the same working environment.

This can make distributed and virtual teams particularly challenging when trying to put Agile practices into play since distributed teams tend to rely more on isolated individuals completing assignments with less team participation and interaction.

And yet, many distributed teams do practice Agile. In order to do this, the team can use a class of tools, technologies, and practices, collectively referred to as "Agile tooling." For example, using web cams to keep everyone connected virtually can help create a sense of common space, regardless of how far apart the team members are physically.

Even if a team is colocated, Agile tooling can be tremendously helpful for the team to share ideas, information, code, knowledge, practice, and workspace. And while software tools may be the most popular example of Agile tooling, other low-tech tools may be used to increase team participation and interaction. These include shared recreational space, daily stand-up meetings, and activities specifically designed to create a sense of team and community.

The point is this: whether the tools are high-tech or low-tech, the goals of Agile tooling are to increase the sense and the bond of team and to encourage participation and motivation among the members.

BUILDING
EMPOWERED TEAMS

Agile teams, by definition, are empowered. This concept is implemented differently across different projects, and it is a significant departure from the way top-down projects are managed. Instead of the traditional "command and control" style of leadership where the team receives orders from someone senior to them, the Agile model consists of a self-organizing, empowered team.

But exactly what is the team empowered to do? It is empowered to make and implement decisions and to add value to the customer. Practically, this means that the team sets the priority of work, the time frames, and even the makeup of the team itself. Each of these decisions should be motivated by how much value they bring to the project. In order to build a properly empowered team, it is important to have the customer or product owner be colocated with the team.

On the topic of building an empowered team, you should understand that, most often, "empowered" means that team members are able to make decisions and to carry out those decisions out in their work. In other words, the way they organize to add value is up to them.

For years, management favored a directed model of decision making where the most senior-ranking people made decisions, and the workers on the team carried them out. Lean management, however, introduced a new model that favors hiring competent workers and pushing the majority of the decision-making to them. By that philosophy, the best person to make the decision is the one whose hands are actually doing the work.

In order to create empowered teams, the following are needed:

- Organizational buy-in
- Alignment with corporate goals
- A shared vision
- Clear communication
- Customer involvement
- Team accountability to the goals they have set

GROUND RULES

Ground rules are unwritten rules about expectations on the project. For example, a team may have a ground rule about what time everyone shows up for work. If the entire team is working by 8:00 a.m. each day, a member who does not show up until 10:30 a.m. for work would disrupt the team. Ground rules may pertain to anything on the project. The important point is that they should be communicated clearly so that everyone knows what is expected of them.

SUMMARY

Agile teams function very differently from the command and control method used on many projects. By facilitating a self-organizing environment, teams are better equipped to solve problems and adapt to change. By locating the entire team in the same space you solve many communication problems.

While they may seem counter-intuitive at first, these self-organizing teams provide the backbone for Agile success.

CHAPTER SIX

AGILE PLANNING

INTRODUCTION

This chapter takes a first look at how an Agile project works. It deals with issues of organization and planning, management, communications, and continuous improvement.

One of the beauties of Agile is that projects constantly adapt to the environment and specific environmental demands. Each of the items covered below may look different from one project to the next; however, this lays out what the various projects and methodologies have in common.

IDENTIFYING THE RIGHT STAKEHOLDERS

Regardless of which methodology a team uses, it is critical that the right people be involved on the project, and that communication flows to the stakeholders.

For the purpose of the exam, you should consider a stakeholder to be anyone with an interest in the project. On traditional projects, the team is considered to be a part of the stakeholder group, but Agile projects treat the two groups as separate.

Stakeholders influence a project, although their role may not be as great on Agile projects as it is on traditional projects. This is primarily due to the fact that Agile projects are more self-contained with the team in its own space and the customer often colocated with the team.

The customer or the product owner acts as the single voice of the users and communicates with other stakeholders. This keeps the entire team from being bombarded by outside requests. The customer or product owner communicates with the various stakeholders, and then takes the items that are in the best interest of the project and brings them to the team.

Stakeholders should have their project-related needs understood early in the project and should be kept up-to-date throughout the project with communication.

ANALYSIS

A myth has evolved in some circles that Agile teams do not perform analysis or planning. This myth projects the idea that the team simply starts coding. Nothing could be further from the truth, although the analysis and planning that take place look very different from traditional projects.

Analysis is all about understanding the problem and the underlying need. If these are not thoroughly understood, then it's very unlikely that any solution will ever properly address them.

Being an Agile Certified Practitioner does not mean that you skip these steps. Instead, you go straight to the customer to get the information first hand. This speaks to the Agile value of Individuals and Interactions and Customer Collaboration. The team may further engage users who can help explain the problem.

Still, while face-to-face conversations (also referred to as high-bandwidth communications in Agile circles) are highly valued, there are times when additional techniques may be brought into play to help with initial analysis.

BRAINSTORMING

Brainstorming is a popular technique used to gather ideas that involves getting input from many participants in a rapid-fire and inclusive environment. Ideas are only evaluated and discussed after they have all been gathered.

It may be implemented by allowing people to speak when they have an idea, which is quickly written down, or to go around the room in a circle, encouraging everyone to participate, until the entire group is out of ideas. The latter technique sometimes helps shy participants to engage.

Agile practitioners like brainstorming because it fosters creativity, and it involves the entire team in the process. Also, each idea is evaluated based on its own merit and not based on who suggested it.

INNOVATION GAMES

Another way to gather ideas and requirements is by playing one or more "games" designed to engage customers or users. Innovation games are actually exercises that involve users.

These games were described in the book Innovation Games: Creating Breakthrough Products Through Collaborative Play by Luke Hohmann. Some of the games that have the most applicability to Agile are described below:

20/20 VISION

In this game, all of the features are posted as cards on the wall to be ordered from most-important to least-important. The facilitator begins with one card and proceeds randomly through the remaining cards until all of them have been put into order.

THE APPRENTICE

One of the team members uses the existing product or manual process, and others observe how she interacts with the system. The team member is expected to make comments or note suggestions as she works with the product with the idea of taking a fresh look at improving the overall process..

BUY A FEATURE

In this innovation game, stakeholders are shown features and estimated prices for their development. The stakeholders have a finite sum of imaginary cash to buy some (but not all) of the features they want, which will help the product owner and the team understand the importance of these features.

PRODUCT BOX

Stakeholders are asked to design a retail box that would entice others to buy this product. They are given materials to design and highlight the features they believe are most important to consumers.

The idea is that the most important features would be featured prominently on the box.

PRUNE THE PRODUCT TREE

The product is mapped out onto the wall or whiteboard with the trunk representing the main functionality and bigger limbs representing larger components, and smaller branches representing features. Users imagine new features and post them on the branches using adhesive notes. It becomes apparent where the bulk of the functionality is located when the tree is viewed. Additionally, branches may be removed (pruned) or reorganized to make them more logical.

ROOT CAUSE ANALYSIS

Root cause analysis looks beyond the symptoms to get to the core issue that is causing the problem.

One way this is accomplished is through Cause and Effect Diagrams. These are also known as Ishikawa diagrams or fishbone diagrams. These charts are used to illustrate how different factors might relate together and to identify a root problem.

Cause and effect diagrams, or Ishikawa Diagrams, are also known as fishbone diagrams due to the way the chart appears like a fish's skeleton.

In addition to cause and effect diagrams, there is the practice of asking "five whys" to discover root causes. This technique, pioneered at Toyota (the birthplace of many techniques used by Agile), looks at a problem and asks "why?", then takes that response

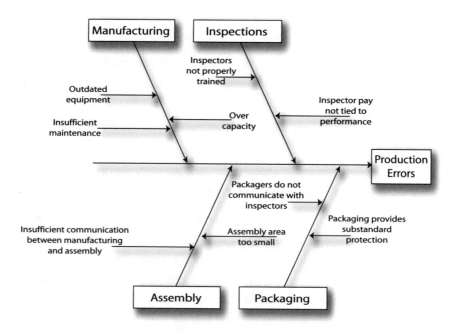

An Ishikawa Diagram Showing Root Cause

and asks "why?" again, repeating five times. Generally, by the fifth iteration of this technique you will have reached the root cause.

As a simple (non information technology) example, consider the following illustration of the five whys:

Effect: The vehicle failed its annual emissions test.

Why? The check engine light was on.

Why? The oxygen sensor had failed.

Why? The fuel injectors had not been properly cleaned, resulting in an improper burn.

Why? The mechanic did not follow manufacturer's guidelines.

Why? The staff was not factory trained for maintenance.

Asking the five whys can help the team get below the surface and understand the real underlying issues at work.

FORCE FIELD ANALYSIS

Not all good ideas are able to be implemented. By their nature, most systems are resistant to change. Force field analysis is one way to analyze that change and to understand the forces for and against it. Once the primary forces on both sides are identified, they are assigned a ranking (by strength) from one to four.

For example, consider an organization evaluating changing their information technology platform from servers they maintain internally to a cloud-based platform.

The force field analysis tool provides an objective way to analyze the forces for and against change to make a more fact-based decision about whether or not and how to proceed.

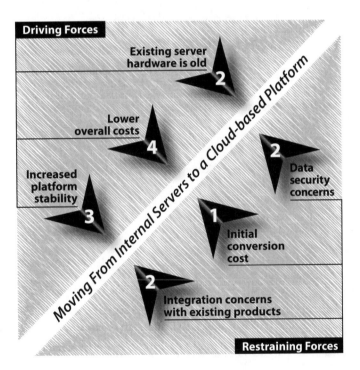

A Force Field Diagram Showing Opposing Forces

PARKING LOT CHART

A parking lot chart is used during requirements-gathering as a way to keep discussions focused and productive. It is usually represented by a piece of paper posted onto the wall.

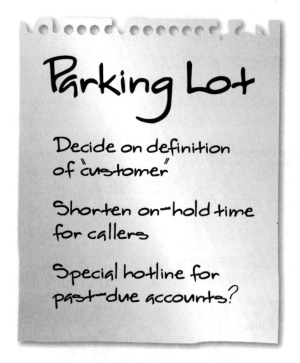

Parking Lot Chart

The parking lot is useful when the team is gathering requirements and one or more of the stakeholders brings up a point that may be important but off topic. The team may choose to "park" the item for the time being and return to it later.

All items in the parking lot should be revisited at the end of the exercise.

PLANNING & ESTIMATING WITH AGILE

ACCURACY OF ESTIMATES

The accuracy of estimates will vary over time on a project. There is a concept often referred to on Agile projects known as the Cone of Uncertainty. The basic concept is that estimates should get sharper over time. An estimate early on the project before most other details are understood will almost certainly be less accurate than one made later by a seasoned team.

CUSTOMER VALUE

Delivering value to the customer trumps most other things on an Agile project. This is an important concept, and because of this focus, it is something that Agile does exceedingly well.

The concept of value is explored throughout this book. For the exam, you should be aware that making decisions based on customer value is a highly favored concept.

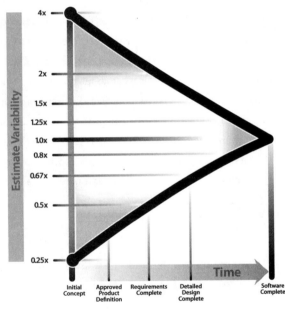

Cone of Uncertainty

PRODUCT VISION STATEMENT

The vision statement is one of the first things that a team (particularly the product owner) typically develops. It is an elevator statement for the product, describing what it is, who would need it, the key reasons someone would pay for it, and what differentiates it in the marketplace.

Sample Vision Statement: For small businesses that need a simple, and flexible point of sale solution, GreatPOS provides a robust, all-in-one retail solution. GreatPOS provides turnkey sales, transactions, and returns on a customizable platform that can be integrated with leading inventory and financial management systems. GreatPOS delivers unparalleled ease, simplicity, and value.

PRODUCT ROADMAP

Stakeholders are not all the same. Some are interested in the overview of the project, others want to know about cost or schedule milestones, while others will want to keep up with the details. In Agile projects, the product vision statement might satisfy the first group, while the release plans and iteration plans will be better suited to the detail-oriented stakeholders, but what about the ones who need more information than the vision statement but less information than the user stories or iteration plans? That is where the product roadmap comes in. The product roadmap is an overview that shows each planned release and the relevant features associated with those releases. The product roadmap is often publicly posted in the team space or in a common, highly visible area. The product roadmap covers multiple releases and may span a few months or even years in time.

Keep in mind that the product roadmap is used as a communication tool that shows the overall plan as it is understood at a point in time. It does not lock the team into a fixed, unchangeable approach. Because of the way Agile projects embrace change, it would be almost certain that the product roadmap would evolve during the life of a project if the project were managed true to Agile principles.

PERSONAS AND EXTREME PERSONAS

It is impossible to design a good product without considering the end user. Teams find it beneficial to stop and consider how the product will be used and look at various usage scenarios. However, not all users have the same needs or will use a product the same way (consider that Viagra started out as a medication to treat high blood pressure).

When considering end users and stakeholders, it can be helpful to create personas to help understand their needs. Let's consider a conceptual point of sale system. End users might be the sales clerk who will ring up the sale, the manager who will ensure all transactions are in balance, and even the customer in some instances. But let's think about this in more depth. The point of sale would likely need to be easy to use for new clerks and trainees, while providing efficiency short cuts for experienced ones.

Agile projects can facilitate this by creating a fictional persona for each role. The personas include a name, a description, and perhaps even a photograph of what the person might look like.

The benefit to creating personas is that when the team writes user stories, they are not simply about a general user; they are about a specific persona. This brings the story to life and helps make it more applicable.

Some Agile practitioners maintain that it is best to imagine extreme characters when creating personas to ensure that as many user stories are imagined and captured as possible. These "extreme personas" can help capture requirements that might otherwise be missed.

WIREFRAMES

One of the ways in which traditional projects may struggle is in the area of documentation. Projects that produce hundreds or thousands of pages of documentation may actually increase risk, which is ironic, given that they are likely intending to reduce risk by documenting everything. The problem is that most people, however well intended, do not read thick technical documents, and even if they do, they may well miss something buried deep within. There have been high-profile disasters and costly wartime errors which were traced back to important details being lost in dense documents or presentations.

Agile projects typically do not produce a lot of project-related documentation, so how are concepts communicated? One important way is through wireframes. On software or information technology projects, a wireframe may be hand-drawn or computer-rendered illustrations showing how the user will interact with the system. Each item is numbered, and system or implementation-related details are commented on according to the numbers.

For instance, if the field on one screen is not editable and is populated from a value in a database, that would be an excellent point to note at the bottom of the page.

An important element of a wireframe is that they are created quickly and therefore may be changed easily. The goal is not to get 100% of the requirements and possibilities documented. Instead, it is to give both the user and the developer a starting point to create a useful system as efficiently as possible.

AGILE THEMES

Themes may be used different ways on an Agile project, but the most common is to assign a theme to an iteration (loosely similar to a short project phase, iterations are discussed in Chapter 8). For example, the theme of the third iteration might be "reporting" or "connectivity," indicating that most of the functionality will center around those items.

EPIC STORIES (CAPABILITIES)

An Agile epic (sometimes called a "capability") is a large block of functionality that may even span multiple iterations. You would expect to find epic stories lower down in the product backlog (the product backlog is covered in Chapter 7). Requirements often begin as epics before being disaggregated into constituent user stories. By the time they rise high in the product backlog, it will be time to break them down into their smaller components.

USER STORIES AND STORY CARDS

Throughout much of this book, you will encounter the concept of stories, or features. In fact, stories are one of the key ways that work is organized and described on Agile projects. But what, exactly, is a user story?

Technical people often think and speak in terms of technology, but the ones using the product tend to think in terms of scenarios. For example, a cashier might focus on a scenario of needing to check out a customer at the point of sale, while a server at a restaurant might consider a scenario of being able to take an order. Both are trying to perform a useful function, and these functions are what we call "features." A feature is something the product can do (or help do), but features can be quite complex. Considering the example of a point of sale, completing a relatively simple sale to a customer could involve:

- Collecting customer information

- Scanning one or multiple bar codes

- Manually entering items, prices, or quantities

- Entering weights or measures for some items

- Scanning/entering coupons and discounts

- Totaling the order

- Calculating appropriate taxes

- Collecting and processing payment

- Generating and printing/ emailing a receipt

In this example, the feature would be completing a sale transaction. This is the useful function. The individual pieces that make this up (represented in bullets above) are the stories. These may not be particularly useful by themselves, but they are necessary in order to create a useful feature.

Each story has to be clear and to demonstrate value. This is key, since they must fit both of these criteria in order to qualify as stories. The stories do not have to be defined in detail at this point, but they do need to have clarity.

Once the features have been defined and stories have been organized around them, the stories are usually written down on note cards, hence the name "story card.". This is simply because the note cards may be passed around, ranked, put into order, stuck on the wall, etc. Putting them on note cards is not a hard and fast rule, but it is a common Agile practice. For projects with a very large number of stories, note cards may become unwieldy, and another solution would likely be needed.

eXtreme Programming (XP) advocate, Bill Wake, describes six attributes of a user story. These are important to know for the exam. These attributes make up the acronym INVEST.

(I)NDEPENDENT: This attribute refers to user stories being mutually exclusive, meaning that they stand on their own and do not overlap with other user stories.

(N)EGOTIABLE: A user story is not a rigid set of requirements. As the user story is translated into reality, it is expected to change and grow. Agile values collaboration, and this takes place between the customer and members of the team. In this context, negotiable means that it is expected to change as it is developed and moves from the developer's hands into the customer's.

(V)ALUABLE: Agile methodologies prioritize based on customer value. When creating a user story, it needs to be viewed from the perspective of the value it will deliver to the customer.

(E)STIMABLE: While Agile teams do not put a premium on precision estimates, they do emphasize being able to generate quick estimates. A user story should have adequate information for the team to be able to estimate the effort involved using whatever technique(s) they employ.

(S)MALL: The best stories are small enough to be useful. Some stories begin as epics (also known as capabilities), but they need to be disaggregated into useful-sized pieces. Obviously this could be carried too far. User stories can always be broken down further, but the most useful ones are easily grasped, estimated, and able to be consumed by the team.

(T)ESTABLE: Good user stories have clearly-defined acceptance criteria. This is the essence of what is meant by "testable." If the story passes the defined acceptance criteria, it will be "acceptable" to the customer.

STORY MAPS

Sometimes user stories (covered next) can be large and unwieldy. It is difficult for people to comprehend very complex and large concepts, and so a time-honored tradition is to break them down into logical components that may be more readily understood.

This is done in traditional project management as well. The Work Breakdown Structure (WBS) is a way of breaking down deliverables on traditional projects; however, do not make the mistake of assuming that a story map is the same as a WBS; it is not. While there are undeniable similarities, the differences are more important for the exam.

DIFFERENCES

Agile Story Map	Waterfall/Traditional WBS
Broken down through disaggregation	Broken down through decomposition
Component stories do not need to add up to 100% of original story, nor do estimates need to add up to original story	Work packages and estimates must add up to 100% of total
Initial node is a large user story or an "epic"	Top node is the high-level deliverable
Typically represented in two dimensions with story cards breaking down the component stories	Depicted in pyramid form

The process of breaking down stories is known as disaggregation. This is where you separate the initial story (sometimes known as an "epic story" if it is very large) into its component stories. In traditional project management, particularly when creating a WBS, it is important that any breakdowns align back to the original node, but when breaking down an Agile story, neither the component stories nor their estimates have to line up perfectly to the initial story.

If you find this confusing, consider that Agile project management puts less of an emphasis on up-front estimating and planning and more energy toward creating and responding to change. Certainly, if done perfectly, the disaggregated components would equal the initial story in content and estimates for cost and effort; however, the effort it would take to get to that level of accuracy would far outweigh any benefits derived from it. Additionally, the first significant change request that affected that portion of the project would stand to disrupt all of that careful estimating work.

FEATURES

A feature is something that adds value to the customer. Features generally require a relatively small amount of effort to implement. They are expressed as "Verb Noun".

For example, the following might be features on a point of sale system:

- Change Sale Quantity
- Apply Discount
- Show Sales Price
- Calculate Sales Tax
- Complete Transaction

MINIMAL MARKETABLE FEATURE (MMF)

A minimal marketable feature (MMF) is the smallest grouping of functionality that can add value to the user, and it is important within Agile. It is larger than a user story but it should be as small as possible. For example, an MMF may allow the user to generate, view, and print a report. Without any one of those functions, the MMF may lack value, but when the three are put together they create value (much like eggs, butter, sugar, and flower create more value when mixed together than they do alone). It is the Customer or Product Owner's job to define the MMFs.

TASKS

Also called "engineering tasks," these are the specific activities the team will undertake in order to add value to a system. One user story for a software product could break down into a handful of actual tasks that span multiple modules of code and which are performed by different team members.

On more traditional projects, tasks may be assigned by senior management; however, on Agile projects the distribution of work is decided upon by the team itself.

VALUE STREAM MAPPING

Agile methodologies are heavily inspired from Lean manufacturing techniques, pioneered at Toyota. It is a way to analyze an entire chain of processes with the goal of eliminating waste. It is intended to give the analyst a deeper understanding of the system by mapping it out. Improvements to the overall system can often deliver great dividends but are difficult to make.

For the exam, be aware that this is a Lean technique used to analyze the flow of materials and information through the system and to identify and eliminate waste.

PROGRESSIVE ELABORATION

The term "progressive elaboration" has been around longer than Agile has formally been practiced. The good news is that the term is perfectly matched to Agile methods. Progressive elaboration simply means that you do not know all of the characteristics about a product when you begin the project, iteration, Sprint, or story map. Instead, the characteristics may be revisited often and refined. For instance, you may gather some of the requirements, perform preliminary design, take the results to the stakeholders for feedback, and then return to gather more requirements. The characteristics of the product emerge over time, or "progressively."

ROLLING WAVE PLANNING

This is another term that has been around quite some time. Rolling wave planning indicates a technique used to plan in stages instead of doing so early in the project. The concept is that details will emerge as the team gets closer to the functionality. By planning, executing, and monitoring and controlling in multiple stages, the details can emerge more naturally.

Rolling wave planning predates Agile and was an example of an Agile-like tool that was often used on traditional projects.

TEST-FIRST DEVELOPMENT

In the history of software development, most of it has followed the pattern of "write first, test later." This seems intuitive, since humans generally like to build things and then inspect them; however, there is a way that turns this approach around.

The philosophy that drives test-first development is that you should have some idea of how a particular software module or feature will be used and that you should begin creating that module with that in mind.

Let's consider the point of sale example again. Suppose you have a function within your application that will total all of the purchases on a ticket. Instead of writing the code that adds up each transaction, test-first development specifies that you create the test cases before writing any code. In this example, we'll specify the following simplified test cases:

SCENARIO	RESULT
Total of sale with zero items. Status returned of NOSALE	PRETAX TOTAL should equal -1
Total a sale with 3 items, valued at $1.01, $2.02 and $3.03. Status returned of VALID	PRETAX TOTAL should equal $6.06
Total a sale with 9,999 items. Status returned of Valid	PRETAX TOTAL should equal sum of each item
Total a sale with 10,000 items. Status returned of NOSALE	PRETAX TOTAL should equal -1

Now that the test cases have been written, the developer can structure the routine more easily, realizing that he or she is developing this to pass a few clearly predefined tests. It's not that these test cases will never change, but it gives an excellent place to begin with the goal in mind.

It is the job of the customer or product owner to define the acceptance criteria that will translate into the test cases. The team's job is to construct the software so that it conforms to the test and not try to make the test conform to the software.

Ideally, these tests should have outcomes of *true* or *false*. Subjective acceptance criteria are usually problematic. When performing these tests, either the module or feature passes the tests or it does not.

THE DEFINITION OF DONE

Building and sharing a common vocabulary is part of working in any field. Different organizations often use the same words and acronyms in varying ways, and meanings are often entirely changed among industries. When different cultures and languages are introduced into the mix, the results can be chaotic.

Agile has its own vocabulary just like anything else, and it's important that words and meanings are clearly understood by the team. One of the most important of these is the definition of the word "done."

A key part of Agile is the idea of represented workflow. Work and workflow should be transparent to the team, but much of that is self-managed. Team members sometimes have to estimate where things are. There is an old joke about writing software that says that the first 80% of the code takes 80% of the time to write, and the last 20% of the code takes the other 80% of the time. That's why in many organizations, progress is often reported at 80% of 90% complete but then doesn't move from that indicator for quite a while. It is a human tendency for things to remain in an almost-finished state.

This is why the definition of done is so important and why it has to be a common definition throughout the entire project team. When an engineer, designer, or developer (or any other team member) checks in a feature as "done," the meaning needs to be clear to the entire team. Work that is almost done may not be represented as done.

The definition of done may be tied to certain acceptance tests, to coding standards, to customer sign-off, or any number or combination of other things.

AGILE ESTIMATION

RELATIVE SIZING

Estimating is a tricky business on all projects, but Agile uses some techniques to avoid getting mired in the process and to keep things moving.

One of these techniques is relative sizing. While it may take on many forms, the idea is to rank stories by their size relative to each other and eventually to estimate based on those rankings.

Imagine a stack of stories written on index cards. Now imagine taking one of medium difficulty and posting it in the center of a wall. Now, the next card will be quickly reviewed and ranked and posted to the left or right of that card based on whether it is easier (placed to the left), or harder (placed to the right) than the one we began with. Each subsequent story is ranked relative to the stories already on the wall, so that at the end, we have an arrangement of stories ranked roughly in relative order of difficulty. The goal at this point is not to be highly precise, but to move quickly through the stack of stories.

The key is that rather than estimating each story from scratch, the team positions each one relative to the other stories, which should be reasonably quick.

Once the cards have all been evaluated, the team will assign points to each story. A way to encourage momentum and not let analysis paralysis creep in is to assign points using the number sequence, 0, 1, 3, 5, 8, 13, 20, 40, 100, or the popular Fibonacci number sequence (similar to the previous sequence). After all of the story cards have been ordered and assigned points, the team can decide how many of these can be fit into an iteration.

Relative sizing is most useful when planning for the next iteration to try and decide which stories can be completed in that iteration.

WIDEBAND DELPHI ESTIMATING

You may already be familiar with the traditional Delphi technique. This technique is used to get expert estimates without the experts knowing who the other members are. This prevents groupthink from developing, and it can keep some group members from lobbying others to get their way. The Delphi estimating technique has been in use for close to 70 years now.

The Wideband Delphi method builds on traditional Delphi. In Wideband Delphi, the team is given estimation forms or cards and is brought together to discuss functionality or user stories.

During the meeting, issues regarding estimating are discussed, but particular estimates or levels of effort are not.

After the meeting and discussion, individuals depart and prepare their estimates. It is important that they do so away from the group. Some permutations of this actually make up a currency to assign rather than try to use actual time or cost. Others use story points, which are measures that only have meaning within the project (15 story points would take more effort than 11 story points, but cannot be directly translated into time without additional work).

Next, the manager gathers all of the estimates and lists them or plots them on a graph, showing the distribution of values but with no names associated with each estimate. Now the team discusses the range and tries to reach a consensus. This continues until the range of estimates becomes acceptably small or a time limit (usually around two hours) is reached.

The advantage of Wideband Delphi is that people may estimate in the absence of any group pressure, while still leveraging the wisdom and experience of the entire group to reach consensus.

As with all estimating techniques, large ranges in the distribution should alert the team to uncertainty and will almost always reflect greater risk.

PLANNING POKER

Similar to Relative Sizing, Planning Poker is an estimating technique used to achieve consensus on work estimates.

Planning poker can begin early in the project, after the user stories have been written. At that point, technical members of the team are brought together for the exercise. It is important that not only one group has input on this exercise. For example, on a software project, not only programmers would work on the estimates, even though they will be the ones primarily doing the work. It is important that analysts, the ones responsible for testing, and any others who have specific technical knowledge about the user story be involved in the exercise.

Planning Poker Cards

Next, each team member is provided with a deck of ten numbered cards. The numbers also follow a modified Fibonacci number sequence of ?, 0, 1, 3, 5, 8, 13, 20, 40, and 100.

As the meeting progresses, the facilitator reads a user story or a functional description. Each of the estimators are given time to ask questions. Then they each select a card that represents the relative level of effort for this story, but they do not show their card to anyone else at this point.

After everyone has selected a card, all of the estimators show their cards at once. Then the team discusses the estimates, with particular attention paid to the outliers (the highs and lows). It is often necessary to time-limit the discussions in order to keep things moving, although the discussions are a critical part of the process. It is helpful to hear why different individuals may consider something to be very easy or very difficult.

Assuming the estimates had significant variances, the team then performs another round of estimating poker for the same story, followed by more discussion. This continues until the estimates converge or they fall within an acceptable range. Often this occurs after about three rounds, but it may take more than that.

Planning poker works well with teams of about ten estimators. If more than that are involved, things often begin to bog down, and it may be best to divide the team into groups.

AFFINITY ESTIMATING

Estimating is a function of planning, and one of the concepts of Agile is that too much planning can quickly become counter-productive. Trying to estimate a large number of user stories or features very precisely can consume so many resources that it actually causes the project to finish later than it would if the team simply made a quicker pass at the planning and began working.

Affinity estimating is a technique that was specifically designed to address the issue of rapid estimating when the project has a large feature backlog. This is a common situation that projects encounter early on, before much work has been started. Rather than allowing the team to become overwhelmed with the planning task, affinity estimating provides a way to rapidly estimate your backlog.

In practice, there are different ways this is conducted; however, they all have a few things in common. First, the team decides on some kind of ranking or grouping technique. Some teams use popular coffee cup sizes (short, tall, grande, venti, trenta). Others use t-shirt sizes (S, M, L, XL, XXL). Still others use the Fibonacci number sequence or variations presented earlier in this chapter. Finally, each user story is read aloud, and with little or no discussion, the team places the user story within that group or around a sequence number.

Using this technique, a very large backlog of stories may be estimated in a very short time. The process is one that most groups find to be very easy and natural, and what it lacks in accuracy, it makes up for in speed.

IDEAL TIME

Everyone who has worked on a project has likely had the experience of giving an estimate for a piece of work only to find that they did not factor in interruptions and distractions. This can be frustrating for everyone involved in the project, but overhead is a part of every project.

Some teams place less of an emphasis on calendared time (also called elapsed time) and instead estimate based on ideal time. Ideal time is the amount of time it would take to complete something if there were no interruptions, distractions, or meetings.

In a sense this is estimating based on the size rather than the duration. This is because team members are not always in complete control of their environment. Mandatory meetings are called, fire drills break concentration, unexpected illnesses take team members out of commission, and systems experience unplanned outages.

Ideal time is literally how much time a task would take with all the necessary resources at hand and zero interruptions or distractions. It assumes complete focus. While this sounds great (ideal), it is very rare for team members to experience ideal time, except during very brief windows. In his book on Agile Estimating and Planning, Mike Cohn presents an example of a football game, which consists of four quarters of 15 minutes each; however, the reality is that the game is not completed in 60 minutes. Instead, it takes as much as three hours to account for time-outs, commercials, injuries, reviews, etc. Using that example, the football game takes 60 minutes of ideal time but three hours of elapsed time.

The reason ideal time has advantages over elapsed time when it comes to estimating is that teams find it easier to think and estimate in ideal time. It can be very difficult to factor in overhead – particularly if the team is just getting started and does not have a good feel for how much overhead and loss to expect in this environment.

ITERATION & RELEASE PLANNING

As we take a look at iteration and release planning, it's a good idea to review these two concepts.

Releases are deliverables of features, benefits, and value to the customer. Releases generally end up in the users' hands. The Agile philosophy is that releases should generally begin early and should continue frequently throughout the life of the project. It may help to think of releases as being more feature-oriented.

An iteration is smaller than a release and is more technically oriented. An iteration typically lasts from one week to one month, and the team works to translate some of the features and user stories from the release into the technical components. The goal is to provide an iteration that can be accomplished by the team in a short time frame and is meaningful to the customer or user. Iterations are of a fixed duration, meaning that the team commits to an iteration lasting a specific amount of time. Further to that point, it is best if all iterations that the team performs are the same length.

There are usually multiple iterations that make up a single release, and most of these iterations are roughly the same length. On many projects, the first iteration is Iteration 0 (zero), which is primarily a planning iteration (recall that the charter is sometimes written as part of Iteration 0); and the last iteration within a release may be referred to as Iteration H, which is a hardening iteration where no new features are implemented but all of the functionality that is in the release is thoroughly tested and reliability is ensured. If the team includes a hardening iteration, there will be an empty iteration backlog at the start of that iteration.

Now let's look at how a release plan is created. The release plan is generally driven by the customer or product owner. Usually teams have either a customer or a product owner working as part of their team, but not both. (We'll look at roles more carefully in Chapter 9). The product owner will look at the overall end product and will attempt to lay out how functionality might be grouped in meaningful stages, or releases. But this process will benefit greatly from team involvement as well. Because of their technical expertise, the team may help the product owner improve the release plan so that it is more realistic.

In general, the product owner will group functionality together in a way that produces the most value, and while the team should have input, this is primarily the product owner's responsibility. Constraints and milestones will need to be considered, along with functional and technical considerations.

It is important to stress that a release plan is neither an edict by the product owner nor a firm contract with the team. It is a plan, and plans can be very fluid in the Agile world. Perhaps the best way to think about it is that the plan should serve the project and not vice versa.

AGILE MODELING

A model is a representation of something else, and Agile modeling is mapping out processes so that the team and stakeholders can review them before they are implemented. The point of this exercise is to map out the desired workflow to understand it more completely. It can include business modeling, requirements modeling, systems analysis, and more.

Agile modeling activities should include the stakeholders so that they understand the model and what it is intended to communicate.

TIMEBOXING

There is a slightly cynical rule in time management known as Parkinson's law, which states that an activity takes as much time as you allot to it. For instance, if you budget for a login screen to take a week, it will take all of that week, but if you trim that down to a half-day, then it will only take a half-day.

The reason is that there is always something else that you can do to make your component or product better, and given enough time, people will fill up the time with that.

Timeboxing is one way of combatting this. It sets a fixed, hopefully reasonable, amount of time to work on features or user stories, and the stories that are completed at the end of the time limit are included.

The benefits of timeboxing are that it sometimes helps the team to focus on the most important features while maintaining a sense of urgency and awareness of the schedule. Time management and estimating are elevated to the highest importance, and there is a strong sense of a start and finish to the iterations.

One downside is that some activities are difficult to rigidly timebox and may result in wasted effort. If someone is 90% complete with a feature, that doesn't much matter under timeboxing. When the time runs out on that iteration, the work stops. Another concern is that the focus can shift from value to the customer to technical difficulty. The team may look at what they can get done more than at what the customer needs.

CONTINUOUS INTEGRATION

When changes are made to one part of a system, they may affect another part in ways that were not expected. On Agile projects there may be numerous people simultaneously swarming multiple tasks, so there are quite a few opportunities for unforeseen problems when these components are brought together. The practice of continuous integration is designed to lessen the impact of this.

In its purest form, continuous integration means that all code changes are checked in and the entire system is built and tested at the end of each day or even more often. Changes that break the rest of the system should be discovered quickly without a significant loss of productivity.

SUMMARY

Some practitioners have argued that Agile projects actually plan more than traditional projects but that it is broken up into smaller pieces and scattered throughout. Regardless of how it compares to waterfall, it's evident that planning is deeply ingrained in Agile. Planning is not as important as a working product, but it is still highly important.

This chapter has quite a bit of content that is important for the exam. The better you know the principles, tools, and techniques laid out here, the better you should do on the exam.

WORKING WITH AGILE

INTRODUCTION

Agile projects implement a series of short, repeatable practices. Now that you are familiar with a few of the Agile basics such as user stories and story pfoints, you are ready to explore the ongoing activities that take place on one of these projects. These include some of the artifacts, practices, and measurements that teams use on a project. All of these items will not necessarily be used on every project, but they are important to have ready when needed, and they are particularly important for the exam.

VELOCITY

We will start this section by looking at velocity. This is a common way of measuring progress on Agile projects. There are several ways this may be done, but in general you need a measure and a unit of time, called an interval.

The point here is not so much to follow a prescribed convention as it is to create a meaningful measure for your project.

For the Y (vertical) axis, you may use any number of meaningful measures of work. This most often would be the number of story points, but it may also be the number of ideal days, or the estimated number of hours. Story points probably work the best for this measurement; however, it is important to note that story points may not be compared in a meaningful way between two different project teams.

For the X (horizontal) axis, you will pick the unit of time most meaningful to you. This is most often iterations but may be calendar weeks or another measure.

Velocity shows you whether a team is getting faster, slower, or is staying the same when it comes to delivering story points. The chart will show you at a glance. While velocity can be an imperfect measure (not all story points are equal), it can be useful to alert you to any team performance issues. Ideally the chart would trend up over time, but if it trends up too sharply in a short time, that may indicate that there was a problem with the original estimates or that the team is working weekends to try to catch up.

Your project's velocity can be a useful tool for future release planning, since if you know the number of story points in a projected release, you can get a quick and rough estimate of how long it should take to accomplish that number by looking at your current velocity.

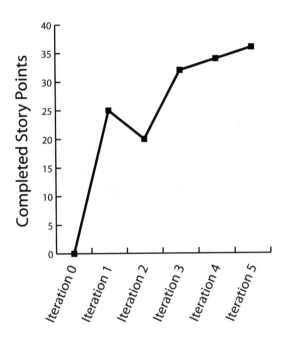

CYCLE TIME

Cycle time, simply stated, is the amount of time it takes for a feature to make it from its start all the way through to completion. The start is most often the point where it enters the backlog, and completion depends on the team's definition of done, but is most often when it exits either development or quality control.

It is an Agile principle that cycle times should be short, and this means that iterations need to be short. Agile is built on the concept of frequent small releases (remember the Minimal Marketable Feature described earlier).

Cycle time is an important measure, and shorter times are more desirable. Quick turnaround of a customer or end user's idea and getting it into their hands is a positive thing. Improved time-to-market also represents a competitive advantage. Another reason short cycle times are better is that Agile projects like to have the customer close to the team. If the team cannot respond to a customer's needs in an effective manner, it creates a kind of distance between the two and robs Agile of some of its benefits.

But while short cycle times are desirable, they should never come at the expense of quality. If the quality begins to drop, then the cycle times are likely too short, and important steps are being missed or skipped. This will likely show up through escaped defects (discussed later).

BURN RATE

Many traditional methodologies try to plan the phase or the project out in detail from the start of the project, but practitioners have come to realize that only near-term activities are easy to plan with great accuracy. That means that estimates created far off or before much information on the project is known are typically not at all accurate.

Agile does not put a lot of emphasis on detailed estimating and in-depth planning, but the reality remains that businesses still need to plan. They need some idea of the value they will receive and how much it will cost them and when they will receive it. That is where the project's burn rate becomes useful. The burn rate shows the amount of cost estimated over a given period of time.

For the exam, think of this as a function of the team's burn rate over time. If a team's combined cost is $5,400 per day, and the next release consists of three iterations projected at 20 days, and a hardening iteration of 22 days, then the cost of labor associated with the release would approach $450,000.

PRODUCT BACKLOG

The product backlog is a list that the team keeps that lists all functionality planned for the project, sorted by value to the customer from highest to lowest. As functionality is completed, it is moved off the list.

The product backlog is mainly the responsibility of the product owner or customer. It is his or her job to add items as new user stories are generated and to clean up old ones. This practice is known as grooming, and it is important that at least every iteration or so, the product owner ensure that the product backlog remains straightforward and relevant.

The product backlog should be "DEEP," which is an acronym standing for:

- **Detailed Appropriately** - The user stories should contain neither too much nor too little detail. They should have enough for the team to begin working to deliver value, but it is expected that the customer will need to be involved to clarify some aspects.

- **Estimable** - The user stories near the top of the backlog should have enough detail to be estimated for story points or ideal days by the team.

- **Emergent** - The backlog grows and changes over time as user stories are completed. It is not static.

- **Prioritized** - The user stories that will deliver the most value should be at the top of the backlog.

ITERATION BACKLOG

The iteration backlog shows all functionality that the team will complete during the current iteration. Functionality is broken down into engineering tasks, and the team self-organizes decides which resources will take on specific tasks.

Unlike the product backlog, which is the responsibility of the product owner, the iteration backlog is maintained by the team. It should be kept in a visibile location for all stakeholders to see.

The link between an iteration backlog and motivation is an interesting one. A backlog that is too large can work to decrease motivation, while one that is too small can have a similar effect. The key is to right-size and prioritize the iteration backlog so that the team can work toward a sense of accomplishment. Frequent releases can help with this as well.

PRODUCT QUALITY

There is no substitute for a good quality deliverable, and anything that disrupts that goal, whether that be bad processes, unhealthy practices, or the wrong people on the team, can have a very negative effect on team motivation. High quality is a motivator, and if quality issues appear on a project, they should undergo a root cause analysis to understand them and correct the underlying factors that contribute to low quality.

ESCAPED DEFECTS

On Agile projects, software is released to the customer rapidly and frequently. While it does get valuable working software into the customer's hands quickly, it also introduces some risks.

Virtually any application is going to have bugs in it. This is as true among Agile teams as it is among any other kind of methodology; however, there should be a process for detecting these errors before they are released to the customer.

Escaped defects are the errors that escaped testing by developers and quality control measures and made it into the customer's hands. If the customer finds it, it's classified as an escaped defect. Obviously, it is a very undesirable outcome.

This is an important metric, and in order to track it, the team needs to have an error tracking and reporting system. If the team notices a sudden spike in escaped defects or a long-term upward trend, then they should investigate the root cause.

FREQUENT VERIFICATION & VALIDATION

Verification is concerned with ensuring that the functionality meets specification, while validation ensures that it does what it was intended to do, and both are performed frequently.

"Frequent" is a concept that shows up quite a bit on Agile projects. Releases are frequent, integration is continuous, and stand-up meetings are daily.

The thought behind frequent verification and validation is very similar to the one behind continuous integration. It is intended to keep the project on track and to quickly detect any deviation from value. By getting the product in the hands of users and testers who will work with it, and by soliciting feedback, the team can verify and validate that the product is working properly and as intended.

AGILE SMELLS

An Agile smell is a term for symptoms of a problem. These "smells" or problems cover the spectrum of any issue that affects the team or the product. There are documented smells that describe issues with the ScrumMaster or Coach assigning work (a bad practice, since teams are self-organizing), problems with team silos (the team should be cross-functional), and people who dominate team meetings and communication, along with many others.

Agile smells are a way to describe and quickly recognize and diagnose common problems so that a remedy may be pursued.

EMBRACING CHANGE

One of the biggest differentiators between traditional and Agile project management is in the way they approach change. On traditional projects, change is viewed with extreme caution, but Agile projects not only accept change, they welcome it! Remember the statement in the <u>Principles Behind the Agile Manifesto</u>, that we "welcome changing requirements, even late in development." The reason behind this is that Agile projects aren't just for the teams. They also give customers a competitive advantage by enabling them to respond quickly to changing conditions.

REFACTORING

From time to time, it is beneficial to reorganize code that has been written. In the Agile world, this is known as refactoring.

Refactoring should not change the code's behavior. Instead, it organizes it more cleanly and in a straightforward way that is more aligned to its intended purpose. This is especially important given the fact that the team has collective responsibility for the code. If one developer writes sloppy code that still works, it makes it very challenging for the team to maintain going forward.

Refactoring is often performed because of a "smell" or because the team recognizes the need.

After refactoring, a complete regression test is required to ensure that the streamlined code behaves in the same way that it did.

INFORMATION RADIATORS

Because of the dynamic and ever-changing nature of projects managed using Agile techniques, communication is tremendously important. One tool to help enhance communication on large or small projects is the information radiator.

The information radiator is a sort of dashboard, posted publicly, that will "radiate" important information at a glance. An information radiator should preferably be posted on the wall in an area highly visible to the team; however, if the team is virtual, it may be necessary to post it online. While the information may be useful for the team, it is also designed to radiate outward to the stakeholders.

A good information radiator will give stakeholders information they seek without the need to ask further questions. This could include information on completed, current, and planned iterations, progress on user stories, current work in progress, and anything else that stakeholders regularly wish to see.

OSMOTIC COMMUNICATIONS

When you work in an environment, you will pick up on bits of information that someone from the outside won't. This is referred to in Agile circles as "osmotic communications."

It is best not to confuse this process with chemical osmosis you learned about in high school. It would probably be better named "diffusive communications," but the idea is simply saying that by spending enough time in an environment, team members will pick up information. For example, if they are all colocated in a war room, they will be able to listen in and participate when discussions are relevant and hopefully be able to tune out when they are not.

By this time you should understand that the whole Agile process focuses less on formal, directive processes than on collaboration, and communication should be no different. Instead of a project manager telling people what is going on, information may often be distributed through more informal networks.

Osmotic communication can also be a useful technique for distributing culture, best practices, and helping acclimate members to the project.

On projects with distributed or virtual teams, osmotic communications can be a challenge since the team is not colocated. Some teams use technology as a way to try to replicate the benefits of the war room. For instance, they will all sign into a single chat room using an instant messenger, participate in a group blog, sign into video conferencing software or other collaboration software. While none of these completely replicates the benefits of colocating the team in a war room, they can deliver many of the benefits of osmotic communication.

One drawback to osmotic communication environments can be wasted time, and if the team is undisciplined they may be impaired by irrelevant communication and frequent interruptions. Some teams combat this by setting hours where no one is allowed to talk in the war room, commonly called a "cone of silence."

BURN-DOWN CHARTS / BURN-UP CHARTS

Burn charts are publicly posted graphs that represent the project's status over time. They are designed to communicate a wealth of information about how the project is progressing against the plan at a glance.

Burn-down charts are used on Agile projects to show the progress during each iteration. A burn-down chart will show you how much work remains on an iteration and how much has been completed so far. The idea is that the amount of work will "burn down" as the iteration progresses until there is nothing left. In this example, the Y axis is used to represent functionality, and the X axis is used to show time. As you might guess from the name, you would expect to see a burn-down chart trend downward over time.

A burn-up chart is the exact opposite of a burn-down chart. It shows functionality against the plan, and the progress line would be

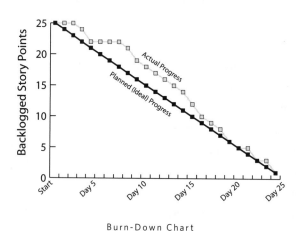

Burn-Down Chart

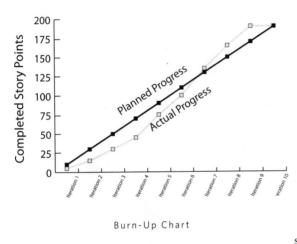

expected to trend upward until it reaches the top right of the graph, showing that 100% functionality has been implemented.

Both burn-down and burn-up charts will be updated after each iteration.

Burn-Up Chart

Both of the examples above work fine if the project scope doesn't change, but project scope almost always changes, and in the Agile world, this is especially true: after all, Agile embraces change.

These charts offer an outstanding visual representation of progress over time.

KANBAN BOARD
(TASK BOARD)

Kanban is a term that originated with Lean Manufacturing, where it is used to provide information to the production line that they can use to respond. The word "Kanban" is a Japanese term that literally means "signal" in English.

In Kanban, a workflow is defined for user stories (e.g., plan, do, check, done), and as user stories are "pulled" through the system, they pull new work from the backlog.

Agile applies this concept by giving information in the form of Kanban boards, or charts, that deliver information to the team. The goal is to help the team members manage their work and respond to the project as it progresses.

The term "Kanban board" refers to a specific task board that the team and other stakeholders can see. It will be posted in the team's war room or another highly visible

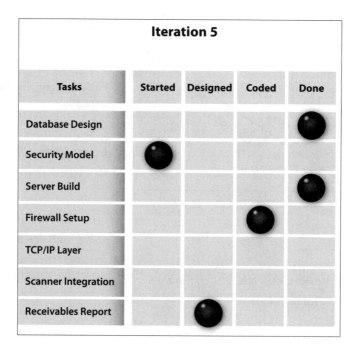

Kanban Board

area and will allow people to see how the project is progressing at a glance. Additionally, team members will be responsible for updating this board themselves. They may do this by making a note, coloring a box, or physically moving a marker or token along as they complete tasks.

An important point to note here is that the Kanban board represents work in progress (WIP), and one of its purposes is to help the team limit WIP. These WIP limits are important, because they help the team to focus on doing a few things correctly and not having too much going on at one time. Kanban boards show all WIP at one time, which may be used as a tool to help discourage too much work in the system at once.

A Kanban board is a component of an information radiator.

THE PMI-ACP EXAM

EARNED VALUE MANAGEMENT

Simply defined, earned value is a measure of how work is progressing against the plan. In projects that are managed top-down, earned value can be a very useful measurement tool. This is because for earned value managment (EVM) to truly work, the scope must be well-defined, and all changes to it have to be estimated and tracked carefully. Obviously, that is against the principle of Agile, which does not attempt to lock down or carefully control the scope very far into the future.

The problem becomes clear when Planned Value (PV) is calculated. PV is the amount of value the project should have earned at a point in the schedule, but since the scope is not planned out in detail on Agile projects, it's difficult to calculate with any accuracy. They get around this by using the velocity and the team's burn rate to calculate this. Because of this, PV works out to be mostly linear on an Agile project, just like you see with the progress lines in the burn-down and burn-up charts.

This book does not go into many details on how to calculate EVM because it is not relevant for exam preparation; however, there are things you need to understand about EVM as it relates to Agile.

Earned value essentially tracks the actual percent of work complete at this point in time for the total schedule. The issue is that Agile projects often do not know the total schedule, nor is it firmly planned if they do. Agile projects generally cannot give the same earned value measurements as a traditional project could.

When Earned Value is applied to an Agile project it will take the velocity of the team and how many user stories they have completed and will calculate that over the iteration and release plans to come up with an approximate percentage complete.

To the EVM purist, there are many issues with this (again, all stemming from the fact that EVM requires a thoroughly defined project scope). Still, earned value can be calculated for Agile. It should be measured at the iteration level because this is the level where velocity is measured and resources are applied.

Organizational compliance is the real benefit to trying to implement EVM on an Agile project.

CUMULATIVE FLOW DIAGRAMS

Having work in progress (WIP) is essential for any project, but "more" is not necessarily better any more than adding more people to a project would be desirable. There is an optimal flow of WIP through the system, and finding and maintaining the optimal level of that flow is like tuning an engine.

As we have encountered earlier when looking at WIP limits, Kanban seeks to improve focus, quality, and overall project performance by limiting the number of things being performed by the team at any given time.

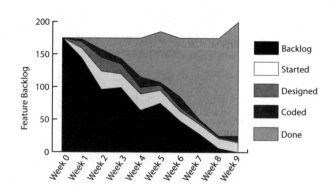

Cumulative Flow Diagram

One way Kanban does (and Agile borrows) this is by representing work in a cumulative flow diagram (CFD).

Suppose, for example that your project's workflow on the Kanban board follows this nomenclature: "Backlog, Started, Designed, Coding, Done."

Because it is cumulative, the chart should convey a strong sense of momentum toward completion that builds as the project progresses. It will also help you spot trends associated with any one of the five components of the chart. For example, if design seems to be taking longer and longer, the project team will want to understand why.

INCREMENTAL DELIVERY

As we have seen, Agile projects do not try to plan everything up front, nor do they try to deliver a solution in one lump sum. Agile embraces a concept known as incremental delivery, and it goes to the heart of what Agile is about.

Incremental delivery addresses a few key Agile points:

- It gets working software into the hands of the customer earlier, delivering value more quickly.

- It allows the customer to work with the system before it is complete, allowing time for changes with less impact.

- It does not try to plan everything up front. Instead, the team can do some planning, deliver some value, gain valuable feedback, and repeat the cycle.

- It prioritizes the most valuable pieces of functionality so that they get in the customer's hands more quickly.

KAIZEN

Kaizen is the Japanese management philosophy of continuous improvement that began in manufacturing and eventually spread to many other practices.

Much like the plan-do-check-act cycle described previously, Kaizen practices creating a plan for improvement, making very small changes, measuring the impact, and repeating. The changes are typically very small, but they can yield tremendous value over time.

Kaizen is strongly aligned with Agile in the way it encourages changes from the workers rather than asking management what should be changed.

SPIKES

Because Agile projects do not try to plan everything up front, they often run into situations where the path has not been determined.

When a development team reaches a "fork in the road," it can bring progress to a complete halt. Worse yet, agreeing upon a process for making a decision may delay the project further.

Agile projects encounter unknown situations at least as often (if not more so) than other methodologies, so they implement a strategy for dealing with this known as "spike solutions."

Simply stated, a spike is an experiment, performed quickly, to help the team decide which fork in the road to pursue. The work is always considered to be "throw away" work, and it only helps the team determine the next steps.

For example, consider a development team that is wondering whether they should use commercially available components for embedding video in an application or whether they should try to write their own. Their primary concern about the commercial version is that it might be too slow, so the team has two of its members to perform a spike. The team downloads a trial version and takes a day to run a series of benchmark tests to determine performance. By analyzing the results, the team is able to determine that the commercially-available component should be within performance limits in only one calendar day.

RISK-ADJUSTED BACKLOG

The product backlog is the primary repository for the features that need to be delivered, and as we have seen, it is prioritized by value to the customer or product owner. This provides much of the structure for Agile projects; however, customer value is not always a sufficient measure. Risk has to be considered as well.

In the world of project management, risk may be thought of as "uncertainty." There may be good uncertainties or bad ones, and both equate to risks; however, it is far more common to plan for negative risk events than it is to plan for positive ones.

Risk management is a rich and complex field. For the exam, be aware that risk is tied to value, and the two must be evaluated in light of each other. If something promises high potential value, it may seem attractive, but if it also has a high risk of financial loss, then the choice will likely be less attractive. If something promises high value but has a very high risk of environmental disaster, an organization would be wise to proceed with great caution.

When the backlog is viewed and adjusted in light of risk, it may take on very different characteristics than one based on value alone.

SUMMARY

In this chapter we began to look at many of the artifacts and some of the vocabulary that Agile projects use. You should now have an understanding of many of the charts that make up a team's Information Radiator and some of the new concepts that Agile introduces. This chapter is undoubtedly one of the most important ones for the exam, so it would be a good idea to scan the headers again the ensure that you understand all of the concepts presented here.

THE PMI-ACP EXAM

CHAPTER EIGHT

COACHING WITH AGILE

INTRODUCTION

Managing an Agile project represents one of the most significant departures from traditional project management. The Coach or ScrumMaster is not there to direct the work, assign tasks, or command and control the project. Instead, he or she should focus on helping the team to embrace Agile and should work to remove any obstacles from their path. The key is that in order for the team to reach its optimal level, it must be self-managing and self-organizing. In this chapter, we will explore some of the approaches, attitudes, and techniques used to coach Agile teams.

THE ROLE OF MANAGEMENT

On traditional projects, the role of management is to ensure that the project is properly planned, executed, monitored, controlled, communicated, and delivered. The manager constantly monitors the progress of the team and takes corrective action when things do not go according to plan, or if he or she is particularly on top of things preventive action will be taken to avoid problems and negative risks.

As familiar as that may sound, that is the role on a more traditional project. It is not the role of managers, coaches, or ScrumMasters on Agile projects. In fact, the title of "manager" is not used very often on Agile projects. As you have seen by now, Agile is all about the "team."

Managers of Agile projects should allocate most of their energies to managing customer value and helping the team to self-organize. When the team is properly staffed, operating at peak performance, and focused on the value, most other issues will work themselves out.

Successful Agile projects do not just "happen." They are successful because management worked to support Agile principles in the organization and helped to sell the benefits of Agile. It is more than merely switching methodologies. It involves change, and leading change is considered to be the most difficult task most managers ever face.

A successful Agile project not only delivers value to the customer rapidly, but it hits its peak when the team's performance is continuously improving, and the Coach should be focused on this goal.

Another important role of management is to remove obstacles and waste. This is easier said than done. Regardless of how well a team is performing or how long they have been working together, inefficiency and waste have a way of creeping in. Sometimes these may be invisible to the team or impossible to deal with, so it becomes management's function to point them out or remove them outright. Agile wages war on waste and inefficiency.

DAILY STAND-UPS

In case you haven't picked up on it yet, be aware that Agile is a philosophy of management that does not place a high value on meetings. Instead, the value is shifted to executing work, experimenting, and improving the process. The meetings that are held, out of necessity, are generally peer-to-peer and are kept lean, relatively short, and to the point.

With all that in mind, it may surprise you that many Agile projects have a set meeting that occurs every work day. These meetings are called "daily stand-ups," because in most organizations participants actually stay standing for the entire meeting to encourage people not to get comfortable and to keep the meeting as brief as possible. In fact, most projects try to contain these meetings to 15 minutes.

Daily stand-ups typically are held at the same time and place each day, with the entire project team in attendance. If others attend the meeting, they will likely be there to listen but not participate.

At each daily stand-up, the facilitator (generally a member of the team) typically asks each participant three questions:

1. "What did you do yesterday?"

2. "What do you plan to work on today?"

3. "Are there any obstacles or impediments in your way?"

Each team member will answer each of the questions, and, ideally, all undivided attention in the room will be on them. Distractions of any kind should be eliminated.

The purpose is team communication and awareness. It is a good idea for each team member to be aware of what others on the team are doing. This is especially true on software projects that practice daily "builds," or where a project has numerous interdependencies where the work of one person could affect others. Each team member is responsible for their work, and stand-ups help them coordinate.

During the daily stand-up, additional discussions are kept to a minimum in order to make good use of everyone's time. For example, the facilitator should probably not use stand-up time to say "John, that is the third day in a row you've been working on this module. What's the problem?" While a similar discussion might need to take place, it should happen offline, between the team members and John, and it should occur outside of the stand-up. (Ideally in this scenario, John would be feeling some peer pressure to deliver a more desirable update.) The group's time should be valued at a premium and protected from sidebar discussions and distractions.

The role of ScrumMaster or Coach on the team is one that is not domineering or heavy-handed. He or she exists to make sure that the Agile process is being followed and to remove any obstacles.

Daily stand-ups should begin very early in the life of the project and will usually continue throughout, even though the participants may change as the project progresses.

As with every other activity in Agile, the importance is not only the process itself but whether the activity adds value to the project. If daily stand-ups stop adding value, they should be reviewed and probably changed.

ITERATIONS (SPRINTS)

Iterations are at the heart of an Agile project. Remember back to the Principles Behind the Agile Manifesto. In that document it was explained that we "deliver working software frequently, from a couple of weeks to a couple of months, with a preference to the shorter time scale." This cycle, which includes a delivery, is known as an iteration (Scrum refers to iterations as "Sprints").

Iterations are thus named because they repeat throughout the project. They begin with a short planning session, operate for a period of time where the team meets for a very brief daily stand-up, works on the agreed-upon tasks, and ends the cycle with a deliverable of some working software and a brief retrospective to discuss what worked well with the process and what did not. Each Agile release is made up of one or more iterations.

Iterations are performed throughout the life of the project. Some methodologies refer to the initial planning iteration in a release as Iteration 0 and the final, "hardening" iteration which tests and prepares the software for release as Iteration H.

ITERATION RETROSPECTIVES

Most project managers have been involved with meetings at the end of a project where the outcome and the process are reviewed. These go by many names, including post-mortems, lessons learned meetings, and after action reviews. The point of these meetings is to ask a simple question: "what would we do differently on this project if we had it to do again?". On larger waterfall projects, these meetings might even be held after each phase.

When properly conducted, lessons learned meetings can provide important information for use on future projects, but as things tend to happen rapidly and dynamically on Agile projects, it is important not to wait so long to incorporate this valuable feedback.

Agile projects are going to be more fluid than waterfall projects. Instead of planning everything up front, they do the majority of planning as they go or just before the work is performed. The same holds true for lessons learned. Instead of holding these meetings at the end of the project or phase, "iteration retrospectives" are held after each iteration, and the feedback is immediately incorporated into the next iteration. These meetings provide the means for regular, small course corrections for the Agile team.

One of the things that stands out the most about Agile methods is that they are pragmatic. They incorporate what works, and this should be the key focus on iteration retrospectives. In an iteration retrospective (which occurs at the end of each iteration), the team evaluates what worked and what did not. The idea is that the practices are adapted so that the things that worked well are kept, and perhaps even enhanced, while the things that did not work well are adapted so that they add value, or they are discarded.

There will likely be areas or processes identified in these iteration retrospectives that the team can address, but there may be some that are out of the team's control. In this case, the ScrumMaster or Coach will work to help find a resolution. Perhaps the most important outcome of an iteration retrospective is that the feedback be put into an action plan.

Generally, the product owner or customer does not attend an iteration retrospective. It is a time for the team to discuss how the work was performed and ways they might improve their internal process. Consider also that it may be best if the facilitator comes from outside the Agile team (provided that this person is already familiar with Agile methods); however, if the facilitator has worked on the project, it is important that he or she provides a safe environment for the team to discuss the project openly. It is not the facilitator's job to provide answers. Instead, the facilitator should gather actionable information and compile it into a summary.

WIP LIMITS

Limiting work-in-process (WIP) is a concept that has its roots in Lean and Kanban. Born at Toyota, Lean is a way to create more customer value using fewer resources, while Kanban, at its core, focuses on decreasing WIP.

One of the key benefits of limiting WIP is that it is easier for team members to focus on a small number of items rather than a large number, and with increased focus comes the opportunity for increased quality. There are well-documented problems associated with high WIP (just think back to a time when you've had too much work to do at once), and limiting it can actually speed up overall productivity and efficiency.

There is no precise guideline as to how much WIP should be allowed on the Kanban board. It may vary from team to team; however, the important point is that the principle is being followed. Rather than rigorously holding to a specific number of items, set limits and encourage the team to hold to them and increase their focus.

When using Kanban principles, a signaling system such as the Kanban board described in Chapter 7 is used to control how work is pulled through the system. When one item of WIP is completed, another is "pulled" off of the iteration backlog, assuming the iteration backlog is not empty. This should be openly represented so that progress (or the lack thereof) is transparent and visible.

Putting limits on WIP is an important part of Agile. It can increase team productivity and ultimately contribute to higher quality.

PROCESS TAILORING

Some Agile methodologies are more formally defined than others. XP, an Agile methodology discussed later in this book, is a particularly well-defined methodology that also adapts to its environment.

One of the ways XP adapts is through process tailoring. The concept that drives process tailoring is that the process should add value to the project and not the other way around. There is not one process or method that will fit every project, so the processes and methods should be changed to fit the project.

While this looks easy on the surface, it can be one of the most challenging aspects of an Agile project.

STAKEHOLDER MANAGEMENT

As you will recall, stakeholders are anyone who has an interest in the project, whether that interest is positive or negative; however, for this topic, let's consider stakeholders to be people with a positive interest in the project's outcome.

Stakeholders will have varying levels of interest in a given project, and before this can be managed, it should be understood. For example, a person who has a financial interest in a software product will not want the same information as someone who is a user interface expert. Some stakeholders might be interested in coding standards, while others might be focused on design.

One of the activities that helps is a process known as stakeholder analysis. When performing stakeholder analysis, the stakeholders are identified, and their interest in the project is understood. All of this information is captured in a stakeholder register, which is a simple artifact.

If your first reaction is that this doesn't sound like a very Agile-friendly process, think again. It is important that people be involved on the project and that the right people receive accurate and helpful information, and that is nearly impossible without this step being performed. Don't fall into the trap of believing that this process has to be lengthy or overly involved. Instead of trying to list each individual stakeholder, the team may simply opt for identifying groups of stakeholders (e.g., users, investors, operations). A blanket strategy may be employed for communicating with each of these groups.

Typically Agile favors involving the right people on the project, but there is certainly a law of diminishing returns where too many people becomes counter productive. It is usually best to have representatives from each group involved. If the users can nominate a person to be on the team and to represent their interests and expertise, then the whole process becomes much more "Agile."

Once the right stakeholders are identified, stakeholder management becomes a function of communication and involvement. For the exam, favor answers where you disclose more information than you might normally feel comfortable doing. Transparent and open communication should be highly favored.

Along this same line, if you have the chance to involve stakeholders, this should be viewed positively. For example, consider a scenario where your project is having issues with team velocity, while a group of stakeholders is complaining that they are being kept in the dark. If you are given four possible answers, you should gravitate toward the ones that involve the stakeholders on the project. Involving the right stakeholders the right way will help you create the right product, and that is more important than working efficiently and quickly, only to create the wrong product.

Managing stakeholders and their expectations is one of the core responsibilities of any project team. This can become aggravated on Agile projects due to the fact that the project team might seem isolated from many of the stakeholders.

The fact that Agile projects are managed so differently from traditional projects puts them at risk. Stakeholders may have become accustomed to calling all of the shots on a project or to making decisions in a "command and control" manner. The concept of an empowered team might seem threatening or at least unusual.

One key to effective stakeholder management in practice (and particularly for the exam) is to educate them and the organization on Agile principles. The more they understand about how Agile projects work and how decisions are made, the more likely they will be to support the team and the process.

TEAM MOTIVATION

As we approach the topic of team motivation, keep in mind that a sustained, high performance team is the goal. That means that motivation is important from the team's inception until the project is complete. In fact, team building and motivation become more important over time.

There are several factors that go into producing high performing Agile teams. The more important are:

SUPPORT

Support is generally thought of as coming from outside the project, although it can also be from within, and it can have a tremendous impact on team motivation. Support is created when the right people are involved early in the project.

TEAM PARTICIPATION

Agile teams are typically relatively small, with each member expected to make a positive, measurable contribution to the overall success of the project. Teams are cross-functional, which means that everyone can maintain everyone else's code.

The key to team participation is that each team member's contribution is visible to the entire team. The entire team motivation will rise as long as each member is contributing to project success at an acceptable rate.

GROUND RULES

Ground rules are unwritten rules about expectations on the project. For example, a team may have a ground rule about what time everyone shows up for work. If the entire team is working by 8:00 a.m. each day, a member who doesn't show up for work until 10:30 a.m. would disrupt things. Ground rules may pertain to anything on the project. The important point is that they should be communicated clearly so that everyone knows what is expected of them.

TEAM PERFORMANCE VISIBILITY

On Agile projects, having a Kanban board or similar way of communicating workflow and progress can contribute to team motivation. This may also be the case as cycle time drops or velocity rises. The key is to ensure that the team members can see how their efforts contribute to an increase in overall performance.

SOFT SKILLS NEGOTIATION

EMOTIONAL INTELLIGENCE

Emotional Intelligence is a concept that came out of research by John Mayer and Peter Salovey and was brought into public awareness through Daniel Goleman's book Emotional Intelligence: Why It Can Matter More Than IQ. You may see Emotional Intelligence abbreviated as "EQ" or as "EI."

The concept is that traditional IQ tests measure how good someone is at solving problems and at relating, grouping, and associating information; however, some of the world's most successful leaders did not have particularly high IQs. Instead, they leveraged a strong ability to relate to people, to lead, or to work with a team. Conversely, many people have worked for a highly intelligent person who could not manage or relate to people effectively.

High emotional intelligence comes through a combination of elevated self-awareness and social awareness.

A high self-awareness means that the individual knows his or her personal strengths and weaknesses. A high social awareness means that the individual is very aware of how he or she is being perceived by others and has the ability to tailor behavior as needed.

The benefits to a high EI are many. Because so much of an Agile project is accomplished through team effort and consensus, the Coach or ScrumMaster needs to have a strong ability to relate and to negotiate. Abrasive and divisive people, even when technically correct, usually do not make good team leaders.

Possessing and employing a high EI to deal with issues or problems should be highly favored on the exam.

COLLABORATION

The concept of collaboration goes beyond a simple exam topic. Instead, it speaks to the heart of Agile. On Agile projects, people do not operate in silos, nor are most decisions handed down in an authoritarian manner. Instead, most decisions are made in an open, transparent, and where possible, collaborative environment.

Everything about an Agile project should encourage collaboration, including the communication, self-organization, decision making, shared ownership of the code, meetings, and even the space itself. Daily team meetings are "stand up" with the entire team participating. In fact, the space itself is configured so that people can collaborate by having team members sit in open space with few barriers. In many Agile environments, all communication is conducted out in the open for the entire team to hear (and possibly participate in).

The important point here is that collaboration is more than a goal on Agile projects. It is integral to Agile projects to the point that if you have a project that does not have a high degree of collaboration, you should question whether it's appropriate to call it an Agile project at all.

NEGOTIATION

The Agile Manifesto makes the statement that customer collaboration is valued over contract negotiation. To understand this, consider the image of a contract negotiation. Parties are seated across from each other at a table, going back and forth over details while the main project work is likely on hold.

Based on this, you might conclude that negotiation is always a bad word on Agile projects, but this is not the case. In some ways, the concept of negotiation is built right into Agile. User stories are a great example of this. They are highly negotiable for the very reason that they aren't contracts. They do not include every detail of information about a piece of functionality. Instead, they have enough detail to help the team have a productive conversation with the customer, product owner, or end user about the requirements and functionality.

Because the team, users, and customer are highly integrated, negotiation becomes necessary. Agile is not all about letting the customer dictate all of the project priorities single-handedly. Trade-offs must be communicated and understood, and useful functionality must be balanced with time, effort, usability, and technical trade-offs among other things.

This becomes all the more important since, on Agile projects, the scope is also negotiable, and changes are welcomed even late in the project.

The key to remember is that negotiation on Agile projects should not be the adversarial type. It should be the collaborative kind, where the customer or end user is brought into the conversation and helps make the best decision for the project.

ACTIVE LISTENING

The process of listening is traditionally thought of as a passive function. The listener simply sits and listens, but everyone has experienced listening to someone communicating and having no idea at the end what the person said or meant.

Active listening is meant to address this. Instead of being purely passive, it is a technique for listening that involves all parties. The key steps in active listening are:

- Listening
- Understanding
- Retaining
- Actively responding

Someone practicing active listening might listen carefully to the person speaking, giving them full, undivided attention. They might reflect back what was said to ensure they understood (e.g., "just to make sure I understand you, are you asking for us to finish two months ahead of schedule and still remain under budget?"). They might take notes on the conversation to ensure that it was retained, and after listening, they might respond actively (e.g., "I want us both to review the team estimates so that you'll understand why we set the schedule the way we did.").

Active listening can reduce confusion and conflict on teams and can improve performance and results.

CONFLICT RESOLUTION

Projects change the status quo, and this will inevitably create conflict, and resolving conflict on the project has been the subject of much discussion and focus for longer than Agile has been in existence.

When conflict resolution is discussed, one of the terms that is thrown out quite often is "compromise," but this term is not favored on traditional project management and particularly not in the Agile community. The reason is that compromise requires each party to give up something, regardless of who may be right or which solution may be best for the project. It is viewed as a "lose-lose" proposition in the world of project management. Particularly within Agile, the idea of giving up something "just because" is not favored.

One important principle is that the project leader should not rush to try to resolve all conflict. On an Agile project, conflict is expected. This is because the project does not have strong top-down direction. Instead, team members are expected to bring their own ideas, and these ideas compete for merit. Agile projects are more highly democratic, and in a democracy, conversation and conflict can be signs of a healthy, engaged group. Another attribute about Agile teams is that they typically have a greater level of team intimacy than non-Agile projects. This is due to many factors, including the fact that Agile teams are not siloed. The openness of the environment and team dynamics can lead to greater intimacy, which often leads to greater conflict.

If the conflict needs to be resolved, the team leader should focus on communication, letting each side tell his or her story and discuss how they feel. Listening is a big part of the Agile leader's role, and it is even more important since the leader needs to model good behavior for the team. When the leader or coach can encourage or facilitate direct and honest communication, this is best. By keeping the focus on the project and the outcome rather than the personalities, the leader can greatly increase the chances of success.

Teams take on their own dynamic, and as teams grow, the intensity and complexity of conflict may increase. Speed Leas developed a model in the 1980s to describe conflict and to group conflicts into five sections, or levels. An Agile coach may encounter these at any point in the project.

By identifying the level of conflict, the coach may employ different strategies to help the team benefit from it or progress beyond it. The following paragraphs describe the five levels of conflict.

LEVEL 1: A PROBLEM TO SOLVE

At level one, Leas describes a team with conflicting goals, values, or needs. The benefit of this level is that the conflict is based on a problem and has not yet progressed to individuals or personalities.

LEVEL 2: DISAGREEMENT

At this level, the conflict is no longer completely about the problem. In fact, a key symptom of this level is that the problem likely cannot be clearly defined. At this stage, the problem starts to become personal, and self-protection becomes important. Participants may feel the need to be guarded in their conversations, and trust begins to run low.

LEVEL 3: CONTEST

When the conflict reaches level three, it has moved solidly beyond the issues and has become something to be won or lost. The different sides in the conflict are now clearly visible, and they begin to recruit allies to their cause. People begin to generalize about the other side and to project motives that are typically unflattering. At this point, the issues are distorted, and the differing sides will likely disagree about what they are.

LEVEL 4: FIGHT OR FLIGHT (CRUSADE)

At level four, resolving the conflict is no longer the primary goal. The conflict progresses beyond winning or losing to getting rid of a person or people. It becomes an "us or them" scenario, where there can only be one winner. The side with which one identifies becomes all-important. The language becomes all about principles rather than issues.

LEVEL 5: INTRACTABLE SITUATION (WORLD WAR)

The issues are no longer the point. The conflict must be won at all costs, and a win-win scenario is no longer acceptable to the participants. At this level, the coach should abandon seeking a solution to the issue(s) and should intervene and separate the warring team members to limit damage to them and the organization.

SERVANT LEADERSHIP

In traditional project management, there is a healthy debate on whether a project manager should primarily be "hands-on" or should focus on managing the project. In Agile projects, this debate is significantly lessened. The team leader needs to be hands-on whenever this makes sense. He or she needs to model the right behavior at all times.

Servant leadership is a term first coined by Robert Greenleaf. Instead of the top-down commanding leader (i.e., the "smartest guy in the room" philosophy), servant leaders focus on the needs of their teams. They are deeply integrated with their teams (no ivory towers or corner offices here), and they are typically colocated with the team.

Greenleaf noted that the key to servant leadership is that a person is servant first and leader second. Servant leaders tend to be more participative leaders, hands-on with their projects, and involved with the daily activities of their teams.

This philosophy is highly compatible with Agile. It cuts against the grain of hierarchical, top-down management and creates a strong bond between the team and the leader that can translate to greater loyalty.

ADAPTIVE LEADERSHIP

The concept of adaptive leadership comes from research done by Ron Heifetz. The main thrust is that the leader adapts to his or her environment in order to lead most effectively.

Employing adaptive leadership, the leader focuses on activities that add value instead of doing things the way they have always been done. Openness and transparency is highly valued, with communication and networking taking place out in the open.

Job descriptions are more general to recruit people who can embrace problem-solving and adapt to a changing environment. Project policies generally have sunset clauses and may be revisited often. The point is not to serve the policy, but for the policy to serve the project. The flow of information is unencumbered and moves easily on projects where adaptive leadership exists.

Most Agile projects in general, and adaptive leadership projects in particular, function best in a meritocracy where individuals are rewarded based on their contribution to the team and the project, and not on seniority, pay, position, or other attributes.

Adaptive leadership generally works best with leaders who are more seasoned and self-aware. For the PMI-ACP exam, adaptive leadership should be a favored choice. While it is not automatically the correct answer, if you see it on the exam, you should gravitate toward it as a favored choice.

SUMMARY

The differences between Agile and waterfall are evident throughout this book, and this chapter has explored some of the most significant ones. The role of Coach or ScrumMaster differs greatly from that of a traditional project manager. In summary, it is a supportive role, focused on helping the team to become self-organizing and self-managing, while keeping everyone focused on Agile principles. Emotional intelligence and maturity become particularly important when managing Agile projects. Finally, knowing the five levels of conflict for the exam will help when answering questions on conflict resolution.

THE PMI-ACP EXAM

CHAPTER NINE

AGILE METHODOLOGIES

INTRODUCTION

Agile provides a set of guiding principles for managing projects. Many of these principles are general, but the methodologies explored here make them much more specific, each in its own way.

There are numerous methodologies that you may want to consider for actual practice, each with their own distinctive flavor that might be more suitable for your organization; however, for the exam, the list has been narrowed down for you.

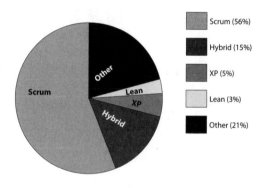

Methodology Marketshare

There are many other Agile methodologies, including the Agile Unified Process, Crystal Clear, Dynamic Systems Development Model (DSDM), Feature-Driven Development, and Kanban just to name a few. All of these have their place in the development world, but this book focuses primarily on Scrum, XP, and Lean. A working knowledge of these should serve you very well on the exam.

According to a survey of 500 self-identified practitioners of Agile, methodology adoption falls roughly along the proportions of the graph at the right.

We'll begin with the most popular: Scrum.

SCRUM

Scrum is an Agile methodology that has been around since the early 1990s. Its primary champions and creators were Ken Schwaber and Jeff Sutherland. You will need to be very familiar with Scrum before taking the PMI-ACP exam.

Scrum is built upon the three pillars of visibility, inspection, and adaptation. All of these refer to both the process and the results. In other words, the work product and the way in which it is created should be transparent and highly visible, should be inspected, and should be adapted frequently.

Scrum is a highly iterative methodology, meaning that activities are performed in short, repeating cycles. While things may repeat, that does not mean that they are identical each time. Rather, the team makes small improvements and changes throughout the project life cycle. These changes should result in greater efficiency and an overall smoother workflow.

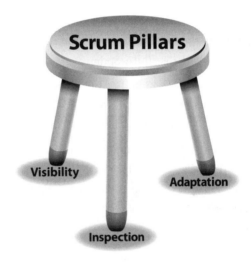

The Three Pillars of Scrum

At the beginning of the project, the Product Owner will present the overall vision for the project. This vision is communicated without unnecessary technical terms. Rather, the Product Owner focuses on "what" the system will do and only gets into "how" it will do it when that is a necessary part of the marketable feature.

The Product Owner will then state the product requirements in a prioritized list called the Product Backlog. The priority of the Product Backlog is initially determined by the Product Owner as what would deliver the highest value. It is expected that the Product Backlog will change, and Scrum embraces change.

The Product Backlog is divided into releases, which are groupings of requirements that go together.

All of the work so far has mainly been organizational in nature. At this point, the Team begins something known as a Sprint. A Sprint is a 30-day iteration that begins with a planning meeting. According to Scrum, a planning meeting can last a maximum of eight hours. This is because all Agile methodologies value results over plans since plans break down with added complexity. Everything cannot be planned out in great detail in eight hours, but that is precisely the point.

This eight-hour meeting is divided in half. The first half has the Product Owner discussing the highest-priority features with the Team. The Team interacts and asks questions about the features and ultimately picks functionality that they believe they can deliver within the 30-day Sprint.

In the second half of the eight-hour meeting, the team maps out the Sprint and defines things down to a task level. The stories that the team plans to complete in this Sprint are placed into the Sprint Backlog.

From this point throughout the Sprint, the team has a daily stand-up meeting called a Daily Scrum. This meeting is constrained to 15 minutes, and as is common with other Agile methodologies, the team works their way around the room with each member answering three questions:

1. What work have you done since the last meeting?

2. What are you planning to do today?

3. What obstacles are you encountering?

At the end of a 30-day Sprint, the team meets for a half-day Sprint review. This meeting is attended by the Team and key stakeholders. The purpose of this meeting is to show the new product functionality while discussing features for the next Sprint.

Every Sprint ends with the team building "shippable" functionality into the product. Although the functionality may not be complete in every way, it should be functional and tested. The Product Owner gets to decide whether this functionality will deploy right away or will be rolled out in a future release.

Before the next 30-day Sprint begins, the Team meets for a Sprint retrospective. In this meeting, the ScrumMaster works with the Team to tune its own development process. Since teams are largely self-organizing and self-managing, they focus on what has worked and what needs improvement and make the necessary adjustments within the Scrum framework. Note that the Product Owner will not participate in these meetings.

SCRUM ROLES

Scrum has a relatively simple structure with three primary roles.

PRODUCT OWNER

The Product Owner is similar to the XP Customer (discussed later in this chapter). The Product Owner has quite a bit of responsibility as the stakeholder representative (typically representing the users prominently), and is the primary liaison to the outside world. The Product Owner will work with a sponsor to ensure the project is adequately funded and will help create the initial backlog of features and a release plan.

The Product Owner writes the user stories and has primary responsibility for the product backlog and for grooming and prioritizing it. He or she will also meet with the team for the first half of an iteration planning meeting to discuss the user stories from a functionality perspective.

TEAM

On a Scrum project, teams are self-organizing and self-managing, and their primary job is to develop the product. Ideally, team members are highly interchangeable (i.e., generalists rather than specialists). The team is ultimately responsible for the results.

SCRUMMASTER

The ScrumMaster is the person responsible for helping the team to follow the Scrum process. When a new team member joins, the ScrumMaster helps this person understand how Scrum is implemented on this project. Additionally the ScrumMaster helps integrate Scrum into the corporate culture.

The ScrumMaster should encourage different team members to begin to facilitate the daily stand-up meetings rather than facilitating it himself or herself.

XP

XP is an Agile methodology developed by Kent Beck. It is one of the more disciplined Agile approaches, pushing members of the team and the customer to stay highly-focused.

Customers initially define the application features with user stories. While the concept of user stories varies somewhat among Agile practitioners (and even among XP practitioners), the overall goal is the same. The user story captures small scenarios about how it is envisioned that the users will interact with the system. It is the customer's primary responsibility to define the user stories, and it is common for new and updated stories to be introduced throughout the project.

The team members work to break these user stories down into story points. There is also quite a lot of variance to story points among XP teams, but story points are not intended to be particularly accurate. Instead, they should give the team an idea of how difficult the particular piece of functionality is.

If a user story is broken down and assigned seven story points of effort, it should represent a similar (estimated) level of effort to another user story with seven story points on the same project, but you cannot easily compare the level of effort between story points on two different projects.

In XP, software developers work in pairs. One programmer works on writing the code, and the other one in the pair actively observes with a focus on the higher-level issues such as integration and functionality. The common analogy used here is having a pilot and a navigator. Most of the time these will swap off regularly.

The number of story points that a pair of programmers can complete in an iteration is known as their velocity, and different pairs of programmers on the same team will often have different velocities. These pair velocities may be aggregated to calculate a team velocity.

Story points may have a numeric estimate, or they may be assigned to categories such as clothing sizes or even coffee drink sizes. One common measure is the Fibonacci number sequence. The idea is to create a relative scale to show that helps communicate that one user story with a given number of story points will be roughly similar in effort to another user story with the same number of points on the same project.

On XP projects, iterations are generally shorter than the typical Scrum iteration. When using XP, an iteration will vary between one and three weeks, and the duration of subsequent iterations will stay fixed throughout the project. In other words, teams that use one week iterations will generally stay with that for each iteration on the project. This shorter iteration cycle is more evidence for how the team must be disciplined. To complete an entire iteration within a single week requires the team and the customer to stay highly focused and eliminate all distractions.

At the start of each iteration, the team and the customer will meet to discuss the user stories and features that the customer wants to see. The team will begin to break these down into specific tasks and will then agree on who will work on the tasks. The developers will then estimate the effort by assigning story points. One principle in XP is that a team member cannot take on more story points in the current iteration than he or she was able to complete in the last iteration.

After the planning meeting, where work is agreed upon and estimated, the programmers work in pairs to write the test cases. This is known as test-driven development. Each user story has a series of acceptance tests written that will essentially say that once the system passes all of the tests, it will be ready for implementation. The customer plays a key part in defining the acceptance criteria and the tests. After the tests are defined, the team "swarms" the tasks in pairs to develop them.

These iterations continue throughout the project's life cycle with a working system being delivered at the end of each iteration. These iterations may or may not be delivered to the end users at this point. Since iterations are weekly events, they usually will not deliver weekly updates to the users, but occasionally a completed iteration will be rolled out to the user base.

XP places a premium on high quality software being delivered in every iteration, regardless of whether or not it is going directly to the end users. The short iterations encourage the team to practice efficiency by doing the least amount of work possible and by doing things "once and only once."

THE 12 PRACTICES OF EXTREME PROGRAMMING

There are twelve practices that make up the core of XP. They are:

1. PLANNING GAME.

The planning game is used for each iteration and also for overall release planning. The participation by the customer and the team allows everyone's goals for developing and releasing functionality to be aligned.

The planning game is not a game in the traditional sense, but it is a practice of writing user stories, estimating effort, and committing to a certain number of them for a given iteration. The goal of the planning game is to maximize value.

2. SMALL RELEASES.

The practice of small releases gets functionality into the customer's hands rapidly while allowing for a focus on Minimal Marketable Features (MMFs). Overall this reduces complexity and increases focus on the functionality that adds value. Also, small releases keep the customer engaged more often allowing frequent tuning and response to change.

3. METAPHOR.

The practice of using metaphors means substituting real-world examples for system components. For example, it may help to think of a load-balancing server as a physical line leading up to multiple cash register attendants. The advantage is that it avoids closed thinking about a technical system that may constrain the solution. If the team is completely focused on a load-balancing server, they may not even consider different technologies that might accomplish the same goal more effectively. The risk here is that all metaphors break down at some level if taken too far. They are in place to encourage broad and creative thinking.

4. SIMPLE DESIGN.

XP embraces simple design for several reasons. One is that a simple design more readily accommodates changing requirements. Another is that simple design is the most efficient, and XP ruthlessly pursues efficiency.

5. TESTING.

Software and systems are thoroughly tested on XP projects. In fact, the test cases are written before the actual code to ensure that the program will pass.

6. REFACTORING.

Think of the concept of refactoring as optimizing the source code. There is certainly more than one way to refactor code. One way is to craft it so that the classes, methods, and members all align to the test cases and their outcomes. Another way might be to reduce the complexity as much as possible, including the number of variables. There are numerous articles and even entire books written on the topic of refactoring, but for the PMI-ACP exam, be aware of what it is, that Agile and XP favor it throughout the project, and that the reorganization should not change the code's behavior.

7. PAIR PROGRAMMING.

As described above, pair programming has two developers working on the same code, side by side. When executed properly within the context of XP, combined productivity and efficiency should go up. Paired partners do not have to stay the same throughout the project. Many XP practitioners change them frequently.

8. COLLECTIVE CODE OWNERSHIP.

On traditional projects, accountability is important, and this is usually achieved by giving responsibility to one programmer or a pair of programmers for one section of code (typically that he or she wrote). Under XP, however, responsibility and accountability are distributed to the team so that the entire team is collectively responsible for all of the code.

9. CONTINUOUS INTEGRATION.

The concept of continuous integration is very straightforward: each new engineering task or component that a pair works on is integrated back into the system as soon as possible. Because iterations are very short in XP, this often occurs several times per day. The advantages to this are that the team is constantly working with the latest changes from all of the programming pairs, and changes that conflict with other enhancements or changes should be discovered quickly. Each time the new features are integrated into the system, all of the tests are performed against the entire system.

10. SUSTAINABLE PACE.

On traditional projects, it is not unusual for the team to work at a regular pace for a period of time until the project nears some deliverable where the team shifts into overdrive and works increasingly more and more hours. This presents several risks to the project. It is not unusual for team members to quit the project in such times, and defects and quality problems have been shown rise as the team is required to work overtime. XP addresses this with the concept of sustainable pace. Because the pairs are working side by side, the intensity is greater than that of a single programmer working alone. This is why a sustainable pace becomes so important. Rather than work the team harder at crucial points in the project, the team maintains a sustainable, usually relatively intense, pace throughout the project. The pace is also about the hours they work, so that even breaks become predictable. The core idea is that the team should be able to continue at this pace indefinitely.

11. ON-SITE CUSTOMER.

In XP, the customer has two primary responsibilities: to write user stories and to define his or her acceptance tests for the functionality. Being on-site ensures that the customer is readily accessible when questions arise (and they always do). If the customer is not on-site, the team will need to make its own judgment calls, which will likely differ on occasion from the customer's. If it is impossible for the customer to be on-site, then a team member may act as a stand-in for the customer.

12. CODING STANDARDS.

Coding standards include such things as file names, variable naming conventions, indentations, braces, and much more. Different teams may adopt different coding standards within the same organization; however, they should be discussed and agreed upon before development begins. This is important since the team has collective responsibility for the code.

Because not all XP teams are ready for all of the 12 practices, it may be best to begin with only these 6:

1. Planning Game
2. Small Releases
3. Testing
4. Pair Programming
5. Refactoring
6. Continuous Integration

The other, more mature practices may be implemented as the team matures and adapts to XP.

XP ROLES

XP COACH

In XP, the Coach is the one who makes sure the team adheres to the XP process and helps the team get better. XP is a disciplined methodology, and the Coach will likely take a more active role in making sure that XP principles are followed.

Since the team is expected to continuously learn and get better, the Coach helps point out learning opportunities.

The Coach should be a supporting role on XP projects and not a top-down leader.

XP CUSTOMER

The XP Customer is the product expert. He or she makes sure the right product is built and gives input as to the order in which features would deliver the greatest value. Also, the Customer participates with the team in a planning game to help determine in what order the features will be developed.

The Customer also determines the acceptance criteria and tests for the work so that the team is able to determine whether or not something is "done."

XP PROGRAMMER

XP Programmers work in pairs. There are variations in the way XP teams implement paired programming, but one common way is for one programmer to write the actual code while the other one looks on and evaluates this in light of the bigger solution. This method of attacking a problem allows one to pilot while the other navigates.

The XP pair makes up the backbone of the team. They are the self-organizing, self-managing component that pull user stories off of the iteration backlogs and turn them into working software.

While pairing programmers may appear inefficient at first glance, mature and high-performing XP pairs actually report higher performance than if each developer worked alone.

XP TRACKER

The Tracker evaluates and communicates progress against the plan. The Tracker looks at the various plans and plots progress against this. It is most often posted in a highly visible or public place.

The three basic things the XP Tracker will track are the release plan (user stories), the iteration plan (tasks) and the acceptance tests. The tracker can also keep track of other metrics, which may help in solving problems the team is having. A good XP Tracker has the ability to collect the information without disturbing the process significantly.

XP TESTER

The XP Tester helps the Customer take the acceptance criteria and translate them into acceptance tests. The Tester is responsible for executing these tests and communicating the results to the entire team.

LEAN

Lean Software Development was adapted from Toyota and their revolutionary manufacturing program. It has seven basic principles that have been applied to software development. They are:

1. ELIMINATE WASTE

While no Agile practice encourages waste or inefficiency, Lean is ruthless about eliminating it. Waste may take on many forms. It may be in the form of excessive meeting, planning, documentation, testing, or any function. The key question is: could we have achieved a positive result without doing this step? If the answer is "yes," then it should be eliminated. Lean makes use of value stream mapping to analyze each activity as part of identifying potential waste.

2.AMPLIFY LEARNING

The pursuit of Lean is marked by continuous learning and improvement, and no matter how good the team gets, there are always opportunities to improve. One way learning is amplified on Lean projects is through shorter iterations and by coupling immediate testing with the iteration. The processes are constantly adapted to make them more efficient and more effective, and brief experiments are encouraged to discover the best way to accomplish something.

3.DECIDE AS LATE AS POSSIBLE

Decisions commit us to paths, yet Agile (and Lean in particular) embraces being adaptive to change. By pushing decisions as far as possible into the future, Lean keeps more options open, which improves the team's ability to respond to change.

4.DELIVER AS FAST AS POSSIBLE

Solid functionality is delivered into the customer's hands as quickly as possible, with the goal of getting feedback and implementing that feedback into the system.

5.EMPOWER THE TEAM

In most traditional (top-down) projects, the manager directs the project and makes decisions. On Lean projects, the team is empowered to make decisions, and the entire team is accountable for these decisions.

6.BUILD INTEGRITY IN

Refactoring is also a part of building integrity in. When refactoring, you are essentially reorganizing the code, and aligning it conceptually with the solution. This is best accomplished as its own task.

7. SEE THE WHOLE

The solution that the team creates should look and feel like a solution and not like ten separate solutions cobbled together. This is accomplished by seeing the entire solution, and this includes more than just the technical components. Seeing the whole also requires that the team understand how the solution is being marketed and even the need that gave rise to the project in the first place.

SUMMARY

It is important to understand the things that make each of these methodologies unique before you take the PMI-ACP exam, but it is also important to know that they are all Agile. That is, the different methodologies presented in this chapter are all branches on the same Agile tree. They each have a different way of expressing the Agile Manifesto and of implementing the values and principles that support it. None of them will contradict the Agile Manifesto, and none of them will violate the principles that support it. Make sure you walk into the exam with a solid understanding of the roles in each methodology and their responsibilities.

THE PMI-ACP EXAM

HOW TO PASS THE
PMI-ACP EXAM

INTRODUCTION

Passing the PMI-ACP on your first try has nothing to do with good luck. It is all about preparation and strategy. While the other chapters in this book are all about the preparation, this chapter focuses on test strategy. It includes techniques on how you can be sure to avoid careless mistakes during your exam.

THE PMI-ACP EXAM

This chapter covers strategies and material related to standardized tests in general and to the PMI-ACP exam specifically.

Before we get into the specifics of the PMI-ACP exam, it would be a good idea to cover standardized exams. Even if you have taken quite a few standardized exams before, now would be a good time to review some important points.

A standardized exam is a test designed to achieve some statistical consistency. Since the PMI-ACP exam is a standardized exam, this essentially means two things:

1. An individual test-taker should perform at approximately the same level on two different versions of the PMI-ACP exam.

2. The results of all people taking the exam should be normally distributed. That means they should form a bell curve.

It is important to know that the PMI-ACP exam pulls from numerous, eclectic sources. As we begin to talk about strategies, it would be helpful to look at how the PMI-ACP exam is actually created. The exam is made up of 120 questions, but as was pointed out in Chapter 2, only 100 of those questions count toward your pass/fail score on the exam. The trouble is that you will not be aware of which questions count and which do not. Volunteers are recruited to write questions, and these questions are then vetted, refined, and tested out before they are added to the exam.

If a question is selected, it may be introduced as one of the 20 experimental questions on the exam. Experimental questions should look like every other question on the exam. The key is that when the results for these experimental questions are evaluated, they should perform like every other question on the exam. Questions that are too difficult or too easy may be discarded.

The topic for each question may cover anything related to Agile, which covers quite a few different methodologies.

There is a common way in which standardized exams are created. Questions will generally fall into three categories:

- Easier questions

- Medium questions

- Harder questions

It is important to note, however, that these questions will be distributed randomly throughout the exam.

EASIER QUESTIONS

Easier questions should be answerable by most test-takers. They generally focus on highly factual topics or ones that require you to choose between an Agile process or a waterfall process. Expect to see approximately 35 of the easier questions on the exam. If you have read this book, you should have no problem answering these.

The best way to recognize one of these questions is that after reading it through carefully a couple of times, you should find that one answer clearly stands out as the most likely candidate.

MEDIUM QUESTIONS

Questions of medium difficulty are the most common questions on the exam. You should expect to see approximately 50 questions that will fall into this category. These questions will cover some of the more challenging topics that will probe your understanding of Agile. In order to answer these questions, you will need to fall back to your study. If you are well prepared, you will find that you can generally trust your instincts.

Medium questions may be recognized by the fact that they should generally be about more esoteric facts. You should be able to narrow these questions down to one or two candidate answers with a bit of careful reading.

HARDER QUESTIONS

The harder questions will generally make the difference between those who pass and those who do not. There may be as many as 35 of these questions on the exam. These will usually focus on obscure practices or nuances of roles (i.e., who should resolve a particular problem). The harder questions on the exam are designed so that only the most prepared test-takers will get them right.

When dealing with the harder questions, it is important to note that most test-takers will not naturally gravitate toward the right answer.

This brings us to an important strategy for strong test-takers. When you recognize a harder question, you should look for the trap and eliminate it first; however, be sure that you are, indeed, on one of the harder questions. Also keep in mind that this strategy may backfire on the easy and medium questions.

Take time to review InSite using the key in the back of this book. The more time you spend, the more you will be able to hone your PMI-ACP strategy.

READING THE QUESTIONS

A critical step to passing the PMI-ACP is to read and understand each question. The good news is that questions on the PMI-ACP exam are much shorter and more direct than they are on the PMP exam.

You will find a few lengthy questions, and on these the best practice is to quickly skip down to the last sentence for a clue as to what the question is asking. Then read the entire question thoroughly. Most of them have a very short final sentence that will summarize the actual question. Make sure, however, to read the entire question at least once! Don't simply rely on the last sentence.

Reading each of the four answers is just as important as carefully reading the question. You should never stop reading the answers as soon as you find one you like. Instead, always read all four answers before making your selection.

A GUESSING STRATEGY

By simply reading the material in this book, you will immediately know how to answer many of the questions on the exam. For many others, you will have an instinctive guess. If you have studied the other chapters, you should trust that instinct. It is not there by chance. Your instinct was created by exposing yourself to this material in different ways. Your mind will begin to gravitate toward the right answer even if you are not explicitly aware of it.

SPOTTING TRICKS AND TRAPS

The exam does have a few trick questions. They are designed specifically to catch people who are coming in with little formal process experience or those who have read a book on Agile and now believe they are ready to take the exam. These people try to rely on their work experience, which often does not line up with PMI's prescribed method for doing things. As a result, they typically don't pass the exam.

At times, however, these trick questions can also fool a seasoned pro! Listed below are some techniques you can use so that you will not fall into these traps.

FOLLOW THE AGILE MANIFESTO

This is always the right answer. There will be questions on your exam that give you "common sense" scenarios that will give you a seemingly innocent way to bypass or contradict the Agile Manifesto. This is almost certainly a trap. The right answer is to fall back on the Agile Manifesto and the supporting documents. Do not give in to any temptation to do otherwise.

FAVOR THE EMPOWERED TEAM

In the Agile world, the team is always empowered. This does not mean that "The Team" is always the right answer, but you should strongly favor an empowered team.

STUDY THE ROLES

By the time you take the exam, you should be confident about the roles on an Agile project. Know which things are performed by the Coach and which ones by the Customer. Know the difference between a Tester and a Tracker. The more you understand the roles, the better.

KNOW YOUR VOCABULARY

Before you go into the exam, take time to review the glossary. The last thing you should do before taking the exam is to read it and then re-read it.

DON'T GET STUCK

You should expect to find a few questions on the exam that you do not know how to answer. You will look at these and see three or four correct answers, making it impossible to pick just one. In such cases, do not agonize. Even using every good technique, you will still have to make an educated guess at some questions. Some test-takers can get quite upset at this, and it can undermine their confidence. If a question stumps you, simply mark it for review and move on. Never spend 15 minutes staring at a single question unless you have already answered all the others. One question is only worth one percent on the exam, so if you do not know the answer, do not obsess over it.

You may even discover that a block of questions seems especially difficult to you. This experience can be discouraging and may cause your confidence to waver. Don't be alarmed if you happen upon several difficult questions in a row. Keep marking them for review and keep moving until you come to more familiar ground. You may find that questions later in the test will offer you hints or jog your memory, helping you with those you initially found difficult.

EXAM TIME MANAGEMENT

You will have a few minutes at the beginning to go through a tutorial. You probably won't find much value in the actual tutorial; however, you absolutely should take it. It will give you time to collect your thoughts and make any notes you want to.

SCRATCH PAPER

You will be given five to six sheets of scratch paper when you walk into the exam. Often this is in the form of laminated, reusable sheets. If you receive these, you will also receive an erasable pen to use with them. You may not carry your own paper into the test. When you sit down to begin the exam, you can write down any particular things to remember such as the INVEST acronym (it's in the glossary if you've forgotten it).

BUDGETING YOUR TIME

You should have plenty of time to complete this exam, even if you are a relatively slow test-taker.

If you have a test time management strategy that has served you well in the past, you should use that. If not, here is a generic strategy that many people have used "as is" to take and pass the PMI-ACP.

- Sit for the tutorial and download any information you would like to on your scratch paper.

- When the exam begins, take the first 60 questions, pacing yourself to take no more than approximately 45 minutes.

- Take your first break. Spend 5 minutes stretching and get a bite of food from your locker.

- Take the next 60 questions, again pacing yourself to take another 45 minutes.

- Take a bigger 15 minute break (relishing the fact that you have now answered all the questions on the PMI-ACP).

- At this point, you should be well under two hours into the exam.

- Perform a review of any question(s) you have marked. Budget for this to take 15 to 20 minutes.

- Start at the beginning, and perform a full review of all 120 questions. Pace yourself to finish this in about 30 to 40 minutes.

This plan will give you plenty of buffer if one of the steps takes longer than anticipated.

MANAGING YOUR REVIEW

When you make a review pass through the exam, you will come across questions that you missed the first time but that are apparent when you look at them again. This is normal, and you should not hesitate to change any answers that you can see you missed. Many people change as many as 10% of the answers on their review. If you catch yourself changing more than that, be careful! You may be second guessing yourself and actually do more harm than good.

When you go through your review pass on the exam, do not take the whole test over again. Instead, employ three rapid fire steps:

Did you read the question correctly the first time?

Did your selected answer match what was being asked?

Perform a complete check of your math in the few questions where it is applicable.

DIFFICULTY

Everyone wants to know what the hardest topic on the exam is. That is a difficult question to answer, but in general it is the questions that present a situation or a problem and ask who should resolve it. You should be able to narrow this down to two choices relatively quickly, but then it may seem very difficult. The important thing here is to know your methodologies and roles!

MANAGING ANXIETY

Finally, if test-taking has always been a fear-inducing activity for you, there is one simple strategy that may help you manage the physical symptoms of anxiety so that your thinking and memory are not impaired: Take a deep breath. This may sound like obvious advice, but it is based on sound research. Studies in the field of stress management have shown that feelings of anxiety (the "fight or flight" response) are linked with elevated levels of adrenaline and certain brain chemicals. One way to bring your brain chemistry back into balance is to draw a deep breath, hold it for about six seconds, and slowly release it. Repeat this breathing pattern whenever you begin to feel panicky over particular questions. It will help to slow your heart rate and clear your mind for greater concentration on the task at hand.

Another thing to remember is that quite a few people who take the exam do not pass – especially on their first attempt. While no one wants to fail the test, you can turn around immediately and apply to take it again (at a reduced rate). You can take the exam up to three times in a year starting with the time you receive your letter of eligibility from PMI.

All in all, reading this book will tilt the odds decidedly in your favor. The more familiar you are with its contents, the better you should do on the PMI-ACP exam.

THE PMI-ACP EXAM

GLOSSARY

ACP

An acronym for Agile Certified Practitioner. A credential managed by the Project Management Institute.

Active Listening

In communication, the role that requires the receiver to receive and understand what is said and provide feedback to the sender.

Affinity Estimating

A technique designed to rapidly estimate a large feature backlog. It uses shirt sizes, coffee cup sizes, or the Fibonacci sequence of numbers to rapidly place user stories into similarly sized groups.

Agile

A set of principles for project management based on the Agile Manifesto. Agile emphasizes self-organizing teams, customer collaboration, rapid releases, responding to change, and the elevation of value.

Agile Manifesto

A document created in 2001 that lays out the guiding principles of Agile projects and methodologies. The Manifesto is organized around four statements that describe the values that Agile methodologies share.

Agile Modeling

A representation of the workflow of a process or system that the team can review before it is implemented in code. Stakeholders and non-programmers should be able to understand and work with the model more easily than code.

Agile Space

Team space that encourages colocation, collaboration, communication, transparency, and visibility.

Agile Theme (see *Theme*)

Agile Tooling

Hi-tech or low-tech software or artifacts designed to increase the sense of team and to encourage participation among the members. Examples include version control software, collaboration software, or video conferencing for distributed teams.

Analysis

Developing an understanding of potential solutions by studying the problem and underlying need.

Artifact

The output of a process or work, typically in the form of a document, drawing, model, or code.

Backlog *(see either Product Backlog or Iteration Backlog)*

Brainstorming

A method of gathering ideas from a group. It is designed to elicit a large number of ideas in a short time frame and to foster creative responses. When brainstorming, participants throw out ideas in rapid fire, and no one is allowed to comment on or discuss a suggestion until everyone has finished.

Burn-Down Chart

A chart used to communicate progress during and at the end of an iteration. It shows the number of stories that have been completed and the ones that remain. The idea is that as the project progresses over time, the backlog of work will "burn down" or lessen.

Burn Rate

The burn rate is the cost of the Agile team, or the rate at which it consumes resources. Most often it is calculated simply by adding up the team cost. It is communicated by the cost per iteration, cost per week, cost per month, or some other measure that is meaningful to the performing organization. If the team "burns" $15,500 / week, then that would represent the team's burn rate.

Burn-Up Chart

The opposite of a burn down chart, showing functionality completed over time. Progress trends up as stories are completed and value is accumulated.

Burn up charts do not show work-in-progress, so it is not an accurate way to predict the end of the project.

Capability *(see Epic)*

Cause and Effect Diagram *(see Root Cause Diagram)*

Ceremony

> A regular meeting on an Agile project such as the iteration planning meeting, the daily stand-up, the iteration review, and the iteration retrospective.

Change

> On Agile projects, this most often refers to changing requirements. Agile embraces changing requirements, even if they occur late in the project, viewing it as a competitive advantage the team can give to the customer.

Charter

> The document that formally begins the project. Charters are created in the project's initiation, and they include the project's justification, a summary-level budget, the major milestones, critical success factors, constraints, assumptions, and authorization for the team to begin working.

Chicken

> Someone on an Agile project who is involved but not committed *(see also Pig)*. Chickens should not be part of the core project team but may have input.

Coach

> In the eXtreme Programming (XP) methodology, the Coach is the person who keeps the team focused on learning and the XP processes. The Coach embodies the XP values and will help the team deliver value while improving.

Collaboration

> Working together toward a common goal.

Collective Code Ownership

> An environment where the entire team is collectively responsible for 100% of the code. This means that each member of the team is cross-capable of maintaining everyone else's code. Collective Code Ownership discourages specialization and the formation of silos.

Colocation

Having the entire team physically working in one room.

Command and Control

A non-Agile principle where decisions are made by individuals higher up on the organizational chart and are handed down to the team.

Communication

Information shared. On Agile teams, communication should be transparent and free-flowing. The entire team should have a strong sense of what is occurring with all aspects of their project.

Compliance

Meeting a regulation. Compliance is one justification for a project to be initiated.

Cone of Silence

Creating an environment free of distractions and interruptions for one or more team members.

Cone of Uncertainty

A term describing the difficulty of estimating early due to unknowns and how that should improve over time. The cone of uncertainty indicates that the ability to estimate should get more accurate if estimates are given shortly before the work is performed.

Conflict

Areas of disagreement on the team. Some conflict is healthy and encouraged on Agile projects, as it can lead to process improvement and a higher quality product.

Conflict Resolution

Working to come to an acceptable agreement when areas of conflict arise.

Continuous Integration

The practice of regularly checking in each team member's work and building and testing the entire system. The most rigorous methodologies do this daily with the goal of quickly catching systemic errors that may have been introduced.

Coordination

Team members orchestrating their work together with the goal of higher productivity and teamwork.

Cumulative Flow Diagram

A chart that is part of an information radiator that shows feature backlogs, work-in-progress, and completed features over time.

Customer

The actual customer or the representative who will define and prioritize business value. The customer participates as part the Agile team.

Cycle Time

The amount of time needed to complete a feature or user story.

Daily Stand-up Meeting

A brief meeting, usually held at the start of the day, where the entire team attends and participates by briefly answering three questions: "what did you accomplish yesterday," "what do you plan to do today," and "are you encountering any obstacles?" Daily stand-ups are important to the flow of communication and to the early detection of any issues. Most Agile methodologies firmly keep these meetings to 15 minutes in length.

Decide As Late As Possiblet

The Agile practice, particularly embodied in Lean, that seeks to postpone decisions as long as it is responsible to preserve all possible avenues and make the decision with as many "knowns" as possible.

DEEP

An acronym describing desirable attributes of a product backlog. It stands for: (D)etailed Appropriately, (E)stimable, (E)mergent, (P)rioritized.

Disaggregation

Breaking down epics or large stories into smaller user stories. Disaggregation is similar to decomposition on traditional projects.

Documentation

Something the Agile Manifesto values less than working software. Agile practitioners generally view the right level of documentation as being "barely sufficient."

Done

A term that must be explicitly defined and agreed upon by the entire team. The definition of done is important so that each team member means exactly the same thing when he or she says that a piece of work is "done."

The most common definition of done for a module is that it compiles and runs without error and passes all predefined acceptance tests and regression tests.

DRY

An acryonmy for "Don't Repeat Yourself." DRY underscores the need to maximize the work not done. For example, the statement "This module is not very DRY", would indicate that the code recreates or repeats work already done instead of leveraging it.

Earned Value Management (EVM)

A way of measuring and communicating progress and trends at the current point in the project. If it is required, EVM is best applied at the iteration level on Agile projects.

Emergent

A component of the DEEP acronym that indicates that the product backlog items should grow and change over time as user stories are completed (see DEEP).

Emotional Intelligence

The ability to relate to others and to lead. Emotional Intelligence is not directly related to traditional intelligence measures. Emotional Intelligence is an important leadership skill for leaders to be able to relate to teams.

Empowerment

A necessary attribute of Agile teams. The concept of empowerment on an Agile project means that the team is able to make the necessary decisions to add value. This is in contrast to traditional projects where teams typically have to ask permission or escalate most decisions.

Engineering Task (see Task)

Epic Story *(Capability)*

A very large story that may span iterations. Epics must be disaggregated into their component user stories before they are useful at a tactical level.

Escaped Defects

Defects that are reported by the customer after being delivered by the team. Surges in the number of escaped defects likely indicate a process problem with the team.

Extreme Persona

A team-manufactured persona *(see Persona)* that is strongly exaggerated in order to elicit requirements that standard personas might miss.

eXtreme Programming *(XP)*

A highly disciplined Agile methodology that runs one week iterations and has programmers work in pairs. XP defines the roles of Coach, Customer, Programmer, Tracker, and Tester.

Feature

A word with widely varying meanings in the Agile community, treated as synonymous with Story for the purposes of this book and exam preparation.

Fibonacci Sequence

A sequence of numbers often used in Agile estimating. The numbers are calculated by beginning with the series 0, 1, and adding the previous two numbers together to get the next number, resulting in the following series: 0, 1, 1, 2, 3, 5, 8, 13, 21, 34, 55, 89, 144...

When using the Fibonacci sequence for planning poker or similar estimating methods, it is often simplified as 0, 1, 2, 3, 5, 8, 13, 20, 40, 100.

Fishbone Diagram *(see Root Cause Diagram)*

Five Whys Technique

A form of root cause analysis popularized at Toyota where the question "why?" is asked five successive times, each time looking one level deeper at the underlying problem.

Focus

A highly important team discipline, encouraged through Agile practices such as daily stand-ups, dedicated team space, information radiators, and limiting work-in-progress.

Most Agile practitioners believe it is the Coach or ScrumMaster's job to encourage and protect team focus.

Force Field Analysis

A technique for analyzing the forces that are encouraging and resisting potential or real change and the strength of these forces.

Functionality

In an Agile context, an action that a system performs that adds value to the customer or user. If the user cannot see or experience something, then it does not count as functionality.

Grooming

Cleaning up the product backlog through various activities such as removing items, disaggregating them, or estimating them.

Ground Rules

Unwritten rules that apply to all team members. Ground rules should be communicated with everyone on the team.

Expecting everyone on the team to assemble at 8:00 a.m. for a daily stand-up meeting without being asked would be an example of a ground rule.

High-Bandwidth Communication

Face-to-face communication. It is referred to as high-bandwidth since much of the information is transmitted through body language, posture, expression, and inflection. High-bandwidth communication is a preferred way to communicate on projects.

Ideal Time

The amount of time an assignment would take if there were no interruptions or distractions. Some Agile projects provide estimates using ideal time rather than actual time.

Incremental Delivery

The Agile concept that functionality should be delivered in small stages rather than as a complete solution. The customer benefits from seeing the solution evolve by being able to influence it and learn from it as it develops.

Information Radiator

A group of artifacts that is used to communicate project status to the team and other stakeholders. Information radiators are an important part of maintaining transparency and visibility into the team's progress.

Information Refrigerator

A term used in contrast to an information radiator, to denote a chart that is not visible to everyone and that must be opened up and explored to be understood.

Innovation Games

A group of exercises used to elicit requirements from product owners, users, and stakeholders. Innovation games help frame the process of requirements-gathering in a more creative way.

Interactions

In an Agile context, this generally refers to face-to-face conversations between team members, customers, and stakeholders. The Agile Manifesto makes it clear that "individuals and interactions" are favored "over processes and tools."

Internal Rate of Return *(IRR)*

A way of expressing profit as an interest rate earned. This helps organizations weigh the benefits of alternative investments. When dealing with the IRR, a bigger number is more desirable.

INVEST

An acronym describing the desirable attributes of a good user story. It stands for (I)ndependent, (N)egotiable, (V)aluable, (E)stimable, (S)mall, and (T)estable.

Ishikawa Diagram *(see Root Cause Diagram)*

Iteration

A cycle of work that is repeated on Agile projects. Iterations generally consist of a short planning session, followed by a period of work, and finally a retrospective to evaluate the process and the results and make adjustments.

Several iterations may be combined to form a release, and iterations are repeated multiple times throughout the project

Agile principles state that iterations may last from two weeks to two months; however, the eXtreme Programming (XP) methodology condenses them to one week.

Iteration Backlog

The work that is needed to be performed on a given iteration. The iteration backlog is expected to "burn down" throughout the iteration *(not to be confused with the product backlog)*.

Iteration Retrospective

The half-day meeting at the end of an iteration where the team meets to discuss the work that was done and look for ways to improve the next iteration. An iteration retrospective is focused on process improvement.

Kaizen

The Japanese management philosophy of continuous improvement. After an initial, generally incomplete delivery, Kaizen advocates small, frequent changes initiated by the team.

Kanban

A Japanese management philosophy that literally means "signal." Kanban focuses on promoting visibility of the work-in-progress (WIP) and limiting the amount of work-in-progress the team allows. In a typical Kanban environment, the work being performed by each member of the team is displayed on a Kanban board, which shows the work and its stage of completeness. A team member will not take on a new task until the current one is done, thereby limiting WIP.

Kanban Board

An artifact that shows work-in-progress (WIP). Kanban boards display the workflow stages (e.g., Started, Designed, Coded, Tested, Done) and where the tasks are within that workflow. The team and interested stakeholders can tell at a glance what work is being performed by the team and what stage the items are in. Kanban boards encourage visibility and limiting WIP. *(Also see Kanban)*

Last Responsible Moment

A term indicating that the team should make decisions as late as possible, preserving all options as long as possible.

Lean

An Agile methodology based on the seven principles of Eliminate Waste, Amplify Learning, Decide as Late as Possible, Deliver as Fast as Possible, Empower the Team, Build Integrity In, and See the Whole.

Lean is a highly disciplined methodology that seeks to maximize the work that is not performed.

Metaphor

The practice of using metaphors means substituting real-world examples for system components to help non-technical stakeholders understand problems and solutions. Using metaphor is particularly advocated by the eXtreme Programming (XP) methodology.

Methodology

A specific set of practices, processes, and artifacts that prescribe how a project should be planned, executed, and controlled.

The methodologies covered in this book are based on the Agile Manifesto and Agile principles.

Minimal Marketable Feature *(MMF)*

The smallest deliverable that can add value to users. A single MMF is typically comprised of a group of user stories. By focusing on breaking the project into MMFs, the team can focus on a small set of valuable functionality that can be delivered to the customer quickly.

Negotiable

Part of the INVEST acronym describing attributes of a good user story. Negotiable indicates that user stories are not set in stone. They are malleable and may be challenged and changed as they are transformed from note cards into working software.

Negotiation

Something valued less than customer collaboration in the Agile Manifesto. Negotiation typically involves contracts which can pit the customer against the performing organization. While some negotiation is necessary, it raises the image of contracts and people set at odds, neither of which are valued within Agile.

Net Present Value (NPV)

A way of factoring in the time value of money to calculate a project's worth. Net present value also considers project costs in the equation. *(See also Present Value)*

Osmotic Communication

Communication which occurs as a result of people sitting in the environment. One team member overhearing two other team members conversing in the war room and thus becoming informed would be an example of osmotic communication.

Pair Programming

A practice advocated in the eXtreme Programming methodology where developers work in pairs with one programmer "driving" the keyboard at a time and the other looking on and participating from a different perspective. Under ideal circumstances, pair programming has been shown to be more efficient than having them work as individuals.

Parking Lot Chart

A chart used, primarily in requirements gathering activities, to pause conversations that might distract from the immediate goal. A stakeholder who raises a point that may be important but not necessarily relevant to the current discussion may have the issue "parked" (i.e., written down on the parking lot chart) for later discussion.

All items on the parking lot chart should be revisited at the end of the session.

Persona

An imaginary person or identity created by the team to model interactions with the system in order to gather requirements. For example, if the team were creating a point of sale system, they may create a persona they call "Taylor" to represent a user who purchases large quantities of an item and then returns them for credit later that day. *(See Extreme Persona)*.

Pig

Someone on an Agile project who is committed and is impacted by the outcome
(*see also Chicken*).

Plan-Do-Check-Act

The cycle of work popularized by Deming that proposes that work should be planned,
executed, verified, and adjusted or corrected. Agile implements the plan-do-check-act cycle
in smaller, more rapid iterations than traditional projects.

Planning Game

A planning exercise to create a release plan where each story is estimated for effort by the
team, and using that information, the customer prioritizes it according to the combination
of business value and effort or cost.

The term "game" is used in the economic sense where a game requires players to make
decisions and trade-offs based on the decisions of other players.

Planning Poker

An exercise that has many different forms across Agile projects. Traditionally, team
members individually estimate the effort to program a user story by writing the estimate
down on an index card. Then each team member simultaneously turns over his or her card,
and the discussion is focused on the high and low estimates to understand why the team
member thinks it will be particularly difficult or easy. The team discusses and repeats as
needed until all estimates are relatively in line.

Estimates may be for hours, a number of days, ideal days, or affinity estimates such as XS,
S, M, L, or XL, or points along the Fibonacci sequence.

PMBOK Guide®

The Guide to the Project Management Body of Knowledge published by the Project
Management Institute. The PMBOK Guide is a document that serves as a condensed
guide to the commonly prescribed practices of project management. Agile practices were
largely underrepresented in the first through fourth editions of the PMBOK Guide.

PMI®

The Project Management Institute. Founded in 1969, they are the largest organization of
project managers in the world.

PMI-ACP®

The Agile Certified Practitioner credential, administered by the Project Management Institute. It is designed to demonstrate proficiency in Agile practices.

Present Value *(PV)*

A way of factoring in the time value of money to calculate a project's worth. Present value calculations are very useful to compare one potential project or opportunity with another.

Process Tailoring

Refining Agile processes to fit the project or environment. Process tailoring is based on the principle that the process should serve the project and not vice versa. Agile process tailoring may be performed repeatedly throughout the life of the project.

Product Backlog

All of the known features that are to be implemented throughout the project, regardless of the planned iteration or release.

Product Owner

The Agile project role that represents the customer, users, and stakeholders, and understands and advocates for the overall business value of potential features. The Product Owner maintains the product backlog and also leads the first part of each iteration planning meeting.

Product Road Map

An artifact that shows an overview of current and/or planned product functionality. The product road map will have less detail than the release plan.

Programmer *(XP)*

A role defined within the eXtreme Programming methodology that works in pairs with one person writing the code while another observes and advises.

Progressive Elaboration

An iterative approach where planning occurs in cycles rather than all up front. Projects which use progressive elaboration typically do some planning, some execution, some monitoring and controlling, and then repeat that cycle. Agile projects are highly progressively-elaborated.

Project

A temporary, undertaking to create a unique product, service or result.

Project Management Professional (PMP®)

The Project Management Professional credential, administered by the Project Management Institute. The PMP is considered to be more traditionally waterfall-based.

Qualitative

Descriptive factors that are not measured but still affect product quality.

Quality

Conformance to specifications or requirements.

Quantitative

Factors which are measured (quantified) and that affect product quality.

Refactoring

The reorganization of working code to bring the organization in line with its functionality and make it more maintainable. Refactoring should not have noticeable effects on functionality or performance.

Relative Sizing

Estimating the size of a function or user story based on the size of another one. The exercise of ordering a group of user stories from most difficult to least difficult without actually estimating a duration is an example of relative sizing.

Release

A packaged group of iteration outcomes designed to be delivered to end users and customers. The working software delivered in each release is expected to be highly stable.

Return on Investment (ROI)

The percentage that shows what return an organization makes by investing in something.

Risk

Any uncertainty that may affect the project positively or negatively.

Risk Burn-Down Chart

A chart where the risk to project success associated with each feature is displayed. The project risk will "burn down" or lessen as the project progresses and functionality is completed.

Role

The way in which an individual interfaces with an Agile project. Agile roles on a project may include Customer, Product Owner, Stakeholder, Sponsor, Team member, Tester, Tracker, ScrumMaster, and Coach.

Root Cause Analysis

A technique designed to look beneath the symptoms of a problem to understand the fundamental problem(s) that cause it. Root cause analysis is sometimes aided by Root Cause Diagrams and by the Five Whys Technique.

Root Cause Diagram

A chart also called an Ishikawa Diagram a Fishbone Diagram, and a Cause and Effect Diagram. Root cause diagrams are used to illustrate how different factors might relate together and identify a root problem.

Scrum

A popular Agile methodology developed by Jeff Sutherland and Ken Schwaber. This methodology defines the roles of ScrumMaster, Product Owner and Team and practices daily stand-up meetings with the team. Scrum iterations are known as Sprints. It is built upon the three pillars of visibility, inspection, and adaptation.

Scrum Sprints are preceded by a planning meeting and followed by a retrospective.

Scrum of Scrums

A meeting of multiple Scrum teams, typically attended by the ScrumMaster or a designated representative. In the Scrum of Scrums, each team's progress is discussed, and the work of multiple teams is coordinated. This technique is often used to scale very large Scrum projects where the team must be subdivided.

ScrumMaster

One of three defined roles within the Scrum methodology. The ScrumMaster is responsible for helping the team to follow the Scrum process.

SDLC

An acronym for the System Development Life Cycle. SDLC is a non-Agile, waterfall approach that specifies that projects should be conducted in long cycles with a heavy emphasis on up-front planning.

Self-Organization

The Agile concept that teams should not be heavily managed or directed but should be formed more organically.

Servant Leadership

The Agile leadership principle that states that leadership roles (e.g., Coach or ScrumMaster) function best when they lead by serving the team. Servant leaders do not ask anything of the team that they would not be willing to do themselves.

Silo

A condition where an individual or small group works in an isolated condition with little interaction outside of this effort. Agile projects favor more open and transparent communication rather than silos.

Smells

Symptoms of problems that commonly affect Agile teams and projects. These problems are metaphorically classified as smells, indicating that something does not seem right about the situation.

Spike

A quick experiment used to help the team answer a question and determine a path forward.

Sprint

An iteration on a Scrum project that lasts between one week to one month.

Stakeholder

Anyone with an interest in the project, whether that interest is positive or negative.

Stakeholder Management

The process of keeping the stakeholders up to date, and communicating, and satisfying their needs. Stakeholder management begins with identifying the right stakeholders. Agile projects value engaging stakeholders and harness their expertise and energy for the project.

Stand-up Meeting *(see Daily Stand-Up)*

Standardized Test

A test that is constructed so that the same test-taker will perform similarly each time he or she takes the exam. Standardized tests are designed on a curve to allow only a predetermined percentage of the population to pass. Standardized tests are intended to measure knowledge and understanding.

Story *(see User Story)*

Story Card

An index card that holds the user story *(see User Story)*. The index card format is used to limit the amount of detail and advance planning the team performs.

Story Map

A group of backlogged stories that are broken down and organized by user functionality with the goal of setting the right development priorities.

Story Point

A unit of measure to express the estimated difficulty (effort) of a user story. Story points may be expressed in hours or days or as shirt sizes (XS, S, M, L, XL, XXL), or as a number of the Fibonacci sequence *(see Fibonacci Sequence)*.

Sustainability

A team pace or velocity that can be maintained indefinitely. Agile teams work to avoid a time crunch at the end of an iteration or release and instead try to keep an intense, but steady pace.

Swarming

An Agile collaboration technique where the entire team is focused on a single user story. Swarming may be used for the entire product backlog or simply for a single, challenging story.

Task

Also called Engineering Task. A smaller division of work that may be taken on by one person and generally accomplished rapidly. Tasks are smaller divisions than user stories, and unlike stories, they may or may not deliver value to the customer.

Team

An empowered group of individuals, collectively responsible for delivering value on the project.

Technical Debt

Technical decisions that the team chooses not to implement at this time but that will become obstacles if not done eventually. A team that chooses to implement code quickly even though it does not yet comply with organizational coding standards would be incurring technical debt.

Test-Driven Development *(Test-First Development)*

An Agile-friendly development practice where the acceptance tests for a module are defined before the module is written. The code is then constructed around passing these tests so that it should only pass when it performs correctly.

Tester

The role defined by the eXtreme Programming methodology that assists the customer in defining acceptance tests and then regularly measures the product against those tests and communicates the results.

Theme

The main purpose behind a group of stories, an iteration, or a release. The Product Owner or Customer determines the theme, and the Team agrees on it. For example, a Product Owner may decide that the theme of a particular iteration is "Reporting" or "Connectivity." In such a case, the user stories selected for this iteration would generally be focused around that theme.

Timeboxing

Constraining the project or release by setting a firm delivery date and then working to get as much value and functionality in the delivery as the schedule allows. timebox timeboxed

Tracker

The role defined by the eXtreme Programming methodology that measures the team's progress and communicates it. The team's tracker will measure the iteration plan, the release plan, and tests and will generally post the results in an information radiator *(see Information Radiator)*.

Traditional Management

In the Agile context, a reference to top-down, or waterfall project management, which emphasizes longer cycles of heavy planning, execution, and control, generally with less customer involvement in the team. On traditional projects, teams are managed and are not self-organizing.

Transparency

A value on Agile projects that is implemented through showing what each member of the team is working on and making each person's progress visible to all other team members.

User Story

One or more business requirements that will add value to the user. A user story is relatively small in terms of the effort it would take to implement. They are typically captured on story cards *(see Story Card)*.

User stories are stated in terms of business functionality and not in technical terms. For instance, if the team needed to optimize a database, this would not be characterized as a user story unless the customer requested a performance increase that the database optimization might lead to.

User stories remain fluid (negotiable), even after being written.

Validation

The process of ensuring that the product is acceptable to the customer.

Value

The worth that a project delivers to the business. The quest to add value drives most team decisions.

Value Stream Mapping

A way to analyze a chain of processes with the goal of eliminating waste. It is intended to give the analyst a deeper understanding of the system by mapping it out.

Value Stream Mapping is a Lean technique used to analyze the flow of materials and information through the system and to identify and eliminate waste.

Value-based Prioritization

A practice of letting the Product Owner or Customer determine which functionality is implemented first based on the value it delivers. It may also be applied to the concept of project justification.

Velocity

The number of features or user stories that a team delivers in a fixed iteration.

Verification

The process of ensuring that the product conforms to specifications.

Virtual Team

A team that is geographically distributed. Although Agile projects favor colocating the team, virtual teams are often a reality. Having a virtual team makes communication and many other aspects of the project more difficult.

Visibility

The concept that each team member's work and progress should be transparent to all interested stakeholders. Work and progress are displayed for everyone to see.

War Room

A location where the entire team can work in one dedicated space. A war room helps facilitate communication and a sense of team and avoid silos.

Waterfall

A traditional, non-Agile management philosophy that favors heavy up-front planning followed by long periods of execution and control. Waterfall methodologies are known for being resistant to changing requirements.

Wideband Delphi Estimating

An estimation technique where the team comes together for a presentation on user stories and to discuss the challenges but then estimates in private. The estimates for each story are plotted on a chart with no names, and then the range of points is discussed, and the team attempts to reach a general consensus.

WIP Limits

Limiting the Work-In-Progress *(WIP)* so that the team maintains focus on completing tasks, maintaining quality, and delivering value.

Wireframe

A lightweight non-functional user interface design that shows the major interface elements and how they would interact. Wireframes can give users an idea of how the system might function without the team having to write code.

Work-In-Progress *(WIP)*

Stories or tasks that have been begun. WIP is typically openly displayed on an information radiator, and its progress is shown as it moves through the workflow.

Workflow

A series of agreed-upon stages in development the team follows. For example if a team decided to move each task through a series of stages such as "Started," "Designed," "Coded," "Tested," "Integrated," and "Done," this would represent the team's workflow.

XP *(see eXtreme Programming)*

PRACTICE TEST ONE

This first of two simulated PMI-ACP exam contains 100 questions.
Although the actual PMI-ACP exam contains 120 questions,
only 100 of these are scored and count toward your pass/fail grade.
Your target score is 82 correct or better. Your time limit is 2½ hours.

1. **Which statement best represents why Agile welcomes changing requirements?**
    A. Embracing change in concept will likely reduce change requests.
    B. To give the customer a competitive advantage.
    C. Self-Organizing teams can adapt to changes almost instantly.
    D. Kaizen.

2. **According to Scrum, an iteration planning meeting should last no longer than:**
    A. One hour.
    B. Four hours.
    C. Eight hours.
    D. One week.

3. **Which statement below is true concerning refactoring?**
    A. After refactoring, the software should be more efficient.
    B. After refactoring, the software should be done.
    C. After refactoring, the software should be better organized.
    D. After refactoring, the software should be more effective.

4. **In order to write a feature, a team member needs to get more requirements from a particular user, but the user has canceled the meeting four different times. How should this be addressed?**
    A. The team member should raise this in the daily stand-up.
    B. The team member should bring the situation to the Product Owner.
    C. The team member should escalate the situation to the ScrumMaster.
    D. The team member should flag the feature and proceed to the next item in the backlog if possible.

5. **An example of high-bandwidth communication is:**
- A. A virtual product demonstration.
- B. Face-to-face communication.
- C. A voice over IP phone call.
- D. An email with a multimedia attachment.

6. **Which choice below best defines a story point?**
- A. A unit of measure assigned by the customer.
- B. A unit of measure assigned to the release backlog.
- C. A unit of measure assigned to the task backlog.
- D. A unit of measure assigned to the iteration backlog.

7. **What is a difference between present value (PV) and net present value (NPV)?**
- A. PV considers the time value of money, while NPV does not.
- B. PV does not consider costs, while NPV does.
- C. PV will usually return a smaller value than NPV.
- D. A higher PV is always desirable, but a higher NPV is not.

8. **Which statement is false concerning the project charter?**
- A. It is more applicable to traditional projects than to Agile projects.
- B. It gives the team the authority to work on the project.
- C. It authorizes budget for the project.
- D. It provides milestones that the team needs to consider.

9. **The ScrumMaster's primary role on the project is:**
- A. To manage the project.
- B. To be the primary liaison with the customer.
- C. To measure and report progress to senior management.
- D. To keep the team focused on Agile principles.

10. **Which answer below represents the ideal team size for a Scrum team?**
- A. 4 to 12.
- B. It depends on the initial scope.
- C. 5 to 9.
- D. Any number that delivers maximum customer value.

11. **Which of the following choices is false about team ground rules?**

    A.   They may pertain to anything on the project.

    B.   They should be written by the Coach and approved by the team.

    C.   They apply to all team members.

    D.   They communicate project expectations.

12. **Which choice represents the best definition of a stakeholder?**

    A.   Anyone whose job might be affected by the project's product.

    B.   Anyone who is committed and not merely involved in the project.

    C.   Anyone with an interest in the project's outcome.

    D.   Anyone who engages on the project in any way.

13. **The project's stakeholders are all assembled together. They are participating in an exercise where they are shown features and estimated prices. They use pretend currency to purchase features they like. This is an example of:**

    A.   An innovation game.

    B.   A product-based market analysis.

    C.   Pure product mapping.

    D.   Economic feature enrichment.

14. **A team is analyzing factors that drive change and factors that restrain change. These factors are given numbers that are added up. This is an example of:**

    A.   Root cause analysis.

    B.   Product road mapping.

    C.   Force field analysis.

    D.   Agent-of-Change analysis .

15. **The team is trying to consider how different groups will interact with their product. Which technique might be most appropriate in this situation?**

    A.   Stakeholder analysis.

    B.   Creating personas.

    C.   Root cause analysis.

    D.   Wireframes.

16.   In Agile terminology, an epic is also known as:
   A.   A capability.
   B.   A node.
   C.   An iteration span.
   D.   A root feature.

17.   Which philosophy drives test-first development?
   A.   Creating the test cases first will save time on the project.
   B.   Software should be written in the context of how it will be accepted and validated.
   C.   Developers should be the ones to create the tests that their software must pass.
   D.   Error free software is possible if tests are properly constructed and the code is strictly written to pass those tests.

18.   The team is estimating effort needed to create software. They are placing stories on the wall in order of effort from greatest to least. This is an example of:
   A.   Fibonacci sequencing.
   B.   Planning poker.
   C.   Relative sizing.
   D.   Affinity estimating.

19.   Jerry has just checked in a module of code that was so technically challenging that he is the only person who understands it, nor has he written any documentation to explain it. One of the team members complained, but Jerry has ignored this and has begun working on the next module. What is problematic about this situation?
   A.   Code should not be checked in until sufficient documentation exists.
   B.   All code is collectively owned and maintained by the team.
   C.   Jerry should not have begun working on the next module until the previous one was validated.
   D.   There is conflict on the team that should be dealt with immediately.

20.   If the team is rapidly estimating work by assigning sizes such as 'XS', 'S', 'M', 'L', or 'XL' to user stories, what method are they likely using?
   A.   Fibonacci sequencing.
   B.   Planning poker.
   C.   Affinity estimating.
   D.   Relative sizing.

21. Wireframes may be useful because:

  A. The team can create them rapidly with no code.

  B. They provide the customer with a working prototype.

  C. They can serve as lightweight documentation.

  D. They help the team remove clutter from the interface.

22. Which statement is false concerning timeboxing?

  A. Timeboxed projects still uses iterations to accomplish the work.

  B. Timeboxing helps the team maintain a sense of urgency.

  C. Timeboxing risks shifting the focus from customer value to technical difficulty.

  D. Only the features that are complete when the time limit is reached are included.

23. Who popularized the Plan-Do-Check-Act cycle?

  A. Ishikawa.

  B. Schwaber.

  C. Deming.

  D. Taylor.

24. On Agile projects, unless otherwise indicated, documentation should be:

  A. Nonexistent .

  B. Barely sufficient.

  C. Thorough but not exhaustive.

  D. Enough for someone new to complete your work if you left unexpectedly.

25. Continuous integration means

  A. All code changes are checked in and tested each day.

  B. The team shares a single codebase.

  C. The customer receives all development in real time.

  D. All code should be integrated as soon as it is "feature complete."

26. A small unit that adds value to the customer is known as:

  A. A story point.

  B. A minimal marketable feature.

  C. A function point.

  D. A use case.

27. An iteration would be the same as:

A. A Sprint.

B. A Cycle.

C. Velocity.

D. A Release.

28. Which statement is false regarding eXtreme Programming (XP)?

A. XP programmers work in pairs.

B. XP encourages programmers to take on slightly more story points than they were able to complete in the previous iteration.

C. XP practices shorter iterations than most other methodologies.

D. XP encourages the team to do things "once and only once."

29. If Earned Value Management is practiced on the project, what is the appropriate level to measure and communicate it?

A. Continuous.

B. Iteration.

C. Feature.

D. Release.

30. On an eXtreme Programming (XP) project, a stakeholder is regularly coming into the team's space, taking valuable time and causing minor distractions. How should this be handled?

A. The stakeholder should be invited to join the team and participate as a member.

B. The empowered team should address the stakeholder.

C. Senior management should be brought in to enforce the Cone of Silence.

D. The Coach should take the stakeholder aside and explain XP principles to the stakeholder.

31. Which represents roles on an eXtreme Programming (XP) project?

A. Coach, Product Owner, Programmer, Tester, Tracker.

B. Coach, Customer, Programmer, Tester, Tracker.

C. Coach, Customer, Product Owner, Programmer, Tester.

D. Coach, Customer, Product Owner, Programmer, Inspector.

32. **Which statement concerning iterations is false?**
- A. Iterations should begin early and should continue throughout the life of the project.
- B. One iteration may include multiple releases.
- C. An iteration should deliver working software at the end.
- D. The first iteration is often called iteration zero.

33. **A team is engaged in the activity of documenting a series of processes to understand them better so they can be streamlined. This is known as:**
- A. Flow Chain Mapping.
- B. Systemic Analysis.
- C. Cumulative Flow Diagramming.
- D. Value Stream Mapping.

34. **There are two Agile teams within an organization. Team A has a velocity of fifteen, while Team B team has a velocity of twenty. Management has taken notice and wishes for Team A to take steps to increase their velocity to match Team B's performance. What is the appropriate action?**
- A. Ask the ScrumMasters to cross-attend daily stand-ups so that best practices may be spread across both teams.
- B. Take an earned value measurement as a second measure of performance.
- C. Redistribute team members between the two teams.
- D. Explain to senior management why the request does not make sense.

35. **Lean seeks to:**
- A. Maximize the work not done.
- B. Maximize sustainability.
- C. Maximize story velocity.
- D. Maximize the rate at which value is delivered.

36. **If the product backlog is not up to date, whose primary responsibility is it to address this?**
- A. The ScrumMaster.
- B. The Team.
- C. The Product Owner.
- D. The Sponsor.

37. **Which principle below is least Agile?**
    A.   Incremental delivery.
    B.   Small releases.
    C.   Scalable teams.
    D.   Progressive elaboration of requirements.

38. **Who is responsible for updating the Kanban board?**
    A.   The ScrumMaster as work is completed.
    B.   The Customer, as work is accepted.
    C.   The Tester as work is verified.
    D.   The Team, as work progresses.

39. **How does a cumulative flow diagram differ from a burn-down chart?**
    A.   A cumulative flow diagram shows work-in-progress, and a burn-down chart does not.
    B.   A cumulative flow diagram communicates the addition of new user stories more clearly than a burn down chart.
    C.   A cumulative flow diagram shows individual user stories, while a burn-down chart does not.
    D.   A cumulative flow diagram is release-based, while burn-down charts are iteration-based.

40. **Which Agile methodology is most widely used?**
    A.   XP.
    B.   Scrum.
    C.   Lean.
    D.   Crystal.

41. **The amount of time it takes for a feature to move from inception to completion is known as:**
    A.   Velocity.
    B.   Time-to-value.
    C.   Cycle Time.
    D.   Burn Rate.

42. **The number of story points a team can complete in a single iteration is known as:**
    A.   Velocity.
    B.   Cycle Time.
    C.   Release density.
    D.   Burn Rate.

43. **Senior management has asked the ScrumMaster to calculate the team labor costs for the next iteration. They are asking for:**

A.   Earned Value.

B.   Cost Performance Index.

C.   Budget.

D.   Burn rate.

44. **The customer has reported an error in a software module the team delivered. This is:**

A.   An issue with acceptance.

B.   A problem with validation.

C.   A problem with verification.

D.   An Escaped Defect.

45. **Which choice below most closely expresses the Japanese management term "Kaizen"?**

A.   Signal.

B.   Small changes.

C.   Plan-Do-Check-Act.

D.   Embrace change.

46. **Test Driven Development is characterized by which of the following:**

A.   Test, code, refactor, deliver.

B.   Code, test, refactor, deliver.

C.   Code, refactor, test, deliver.

D.   Test, code, deliver, refactor.

47. **A spike is:**

A.   A small experiment to help the team determine a course of action.

B.   An increase in the number of user stories within a release or an iteration.

C.   A technique used to motivate the team.

D.   A dividing question to assist the customer in the requirements process.

48. **Which of the following is true regarding Iteration Zero?**

A.   The team selects the items of highest value to the customer.

B.   The team attempts to lock down the product scope.

C.   The team typically does not deliver any value to the customer.

D.   The team has a retrospective to discuss other iterations in the release.

49. **Limiting work-in-progress (WIP) is most closely associated with:**
- A. Deming.
- B. Ishikawa.
- C. Kaizen.
- D. Kanban.

50. **The team has a disagreement about the value a potential new feature might provide. What is the right way to resolve this?**
- A. The Team.
- B. The Users.
- C. The Product Owner.
- D. The Coach.

51. **An Agile Coach is involved in negotiations over space for the team with another manager. The Coach is working hard to relate to the manager and to understand her concerns and needs while explaining the team's need for this space. The Coach is using:**
- A. Emotional Intelligence.
- B. Active Listening.
- C. Collaboration skills.
- D. Conflict Resolution.

52. **An organization has just begun to embrace Agile principles. Which would be true about what they would expect to see?**
- A. They should expect project risk to fall.
- B. They should expect more change requests.
- C. They should expect turnover to fall.
- D. They should initially expect more complaints to senior management.

53. **User stories should be:**
- A. Dependent.
- B. Comprehensive.
- C. Negotiable.
- D. High-value.

54.   What is the primary measure of progress?

    A.   Function points.

    B.   Working software.

    C.   The burn down chart.

    D.   The information radiator.

55.   Which methodology would you expect to find programmers working in pairs?

    A.   Scrum.

    B.   Lean.

    C.   Waterfall.

    D.   XP.

56.   In a Scrum planning meeting, who discusses the highest-priority features with the team?

    A.   The Product Owner.

    B.   The ScrumMaster.

    C.   The Customer.

    D.   The Users.

57.   All of the following statements regarding tasks are true on Agile projects except:

    A.   They do not necessarily add customer value.

    B.   They represent the smallest breakdown of work.

    C.   They may be shown on an information radiator.

    D.   They are assigned to individual or pairs for completion.

58.   At the end of a Sprint, how long is the review?

    A.   One hour.

    B.   One half-day.

    C.   One day.

    D.   As long as value is being realized.

59.   Which of the following statements about Agile is the most accurate?

    A.   Agile teams produce fewer issues than waterfall teams.

    B.   Agile teams resolve fewer issues than waterfall teams.

    C.   Agile teams escalate fewer issues then waterfall teams.

    D.   Agile teams are aware of fewer issues than waterfall teams.

60. **Which value is not mentioned in the Agile Manifesto?**
- A. Comprehensive Documentation.
- B. Continuous Improvement.
- C. Contract Negotiation.
- D. Processes and Tools.

61. **The primary purpose of the daily stand-up meetings is:**
- A. To allow the team to coordinate work and communicate issues.
- B. To make the ScrumMaster or Coach aware of any issues.
- C. To communicate progress to the Customer.
- D. To implement continuous improvement for subsequent work.

62. **Product owners do which of the following?**
- A. Prioritize the product backlog, serve as a single voice of the customer, accept the work.
- B. Prioritize the iteration backlog, coordinate team activities with the Coach or ScrumMaster, communicate the value of user stories.
- C. Facilitate daily stand-ups, write the acceptance criteria for user stories, review completed user stories.
- D. Help the team self-organize, explain user stories to the team, help disaggregate epic stories.

63. **A feature was slated to be included in an iteration, but the team has encountered difficulty in getting the software to work. It is time for the iteration to end. How should this be resolved?**
- A. The Team should proceed to deliver software on time but explain to the customer that it does not work yet.
- B. The Team should ask the Coach for guidance.
- C. The Team should deliver the other features in the iteration but should not deliver this feature since it does not work.
- D. The Team should delay delivery of the software until the feature works as intended.

64. **Which statement is true concerning distributed teams in Agile?**
- A. Under Agile, distributed teams are generally as effective or more effective than colocated teams.
- B. Under Agile, distributed teams are generally less effective than colocated teams.
- C. Under Agile, distributed teams follow a different model of organization than colocated teams.
- D. The Agile model does not support distributed teams.

65. Which statement reflects the Agile principles?

   A.   Projects are built around motivated individuals.

   B.   Projects are built around superior requirements captured through user stories.

   C.   Projects are built around the process rather than a product.

   D.   Projects are built around the product rather than a process.

66. The Coach has become aware of an increase in the number of escaped defects. He believes they can be traced back to a single developer. What should he do?

   A.   Address this issue with the team.

   B.   Problem-solve by communicating directly with the developer.

   C.   Post the information in the shared space to raise team awareness.

   D.   Address this issue at the next iteration retrospective.

67. Senior management in the performing organization has asked the Agile team for a detailed project plan. What is the best response?

   A.   Provide senior management with a product roadmap.

   B.   Take this opportunity to educate senior management on Agile principles.

   C.   Have the team produce abbreviated versions of the key components of a project plan.

   D.   Develop an information radiator for senior management.

68. An Agile team's workflow is:

   A.   Developed by the ScrumMaster.

   B.   Represented in the product backlog.

   C.   Agreed upon by the project team.

   D.   The primary contributor to product quality.

PRACTICE TEST

69. **A project team has a velocity of 5. Given the product backlog represented by priority in the table below, what is the best combination of iterations?**

User Story	Estimate
A	2
B	3
C	1
D	1
E	3
F	5

   A.   Iteration 1: AB; Iteration 2: CDE; Iteration 3: F.
   B.   Iteration 1: AE; Iteration 2: BCDE; Iteration 3:F.
   C.   Iteration 1: A; Iteration 2: BCD; Iteration 3: E; Iteration 4: F.
   D.   Iteration 1: ABC; Iteration 2: DE; Iteration 3: F.

70. **Issues that may indicate a common root problem are often referred to as:**
   A.   Hints.
   B.   Symptoms.
   C.   Action Items.
   D.   Smells.

71. **"Prune the Product Tree" is a technique used in:**
   A.   Requirement gathering.
   B.   Release planning.
   C.   Iteration planning.
   D.   Integration testing.

72. **Ideally, team space should be configured so that:**
   A.   Team members face the information radiator.
   B.   Team members have as much privacy as possible.
   C.   Team members face each other.
   D.   Team members can form smaller groups.
   E.

73. **Which question would be appropriate to ask during a daily stand-up meeting?**

    A.   What are you planning to do tomorrow?

    B.   What impediments are you encountering?

    C.   What can the team do to become more effective?

    D.   What can the team do to become more efficient?

74. **An organization's Project Management Office (PMO) has three Agile projects, but each of the projects implements Agile principles very differently. How should the PMO respond to this?**

    A.   The PMO should focus only on earned value management and objective measures and should not be concerned with how the team performs their work.

    B.   The PMO should define how Agile projects should be run within the organization.

    C.   The PMO should accept that Agile is implemented differently on different projects.

    D.   The PMO should colocate all of the Agile projects to allow the groups of teams to self-organize.

75. **When using Earned Value Management (EVM), Agile substitutes what in place of planned value?**

    A.   A calculation using the cycle time and the value of the user stories to be completed.

    B.   A calculation using the return on investment (ROI) for the user stories to be completed.

    C.   A calculation using the velocity and burn rate for an iteration.

    D.   Agile projects do not use planned value in EVM calculations.

76. **On the wall of an Agile project are various items including a burn-down chart, a burn-up chart, a feature backlog, and a velocity chart. These make up:**

    A.   Enterprise Environmental Factors.

    B.   An Information Radiator.

    C.   Organizational Process Assets.

    D.   Agile Tooling.

77. **The most efficient and effective method of conveying information to and within a development team is through:**

    A.   Osmotic communications.

    B.   Using an approved method the team has agreed upon.

    C.   Face-to-face.

    D.   In writing.

78. **The practice of asking "5 whys" is most closely associated with which organization?**
    A. General Electric.
    B. Motorola.
    C. Toyota.
    D. The Project Management Institute.

79. **The Product Owner has indicated that "Feature A" would provide the greatest business value; however, the empowered Team believes that "Feature B" would provide significantly more business value. How should this be decided?**
    A. The ScrumMaster should break the tie.
    B. The Team should make the final decision.
    C. The group should not proceed until there is consensus.
    D. The Product Owner should be the one to decide.

80. **Which of the following attributes should be applicable to User Stories?**
    A. Validated, Economical.
    B. Verifiable, Editable.
    C. Valuable, Estimable.
    D. Vital, Elastic.

81. **The Agile Manifesto was created in which year?**
    A. 2001.
    B. 1989.
    C. 1996.
    D. 2006.

82. **In which of the following ways is Agile project management like waterfall project management?**
    A. Both welcome changing requirements.
    B. Both practice short cycles or iterations.
    C. Both divide the project up into phases.
    D. Both perform analysis and planning.

83. **The team has been using personas for the past two days on the project. On day three, someone suggests that they switch to extreme personas. Why might this make sense?**
    A. Extreme personas can help eliminate waste.
    B. Extreme personas can help elicit requirements that regular personas might miss.
    C. Extreme personas can help move the team beyond conflict.
    D. Extreme personas can help introduce healthy conflict into the team.

84. **The purpose of an iteration retrospective is:**

A. To analyze the release and determine what could have been improved.

B. To provide an opportunity for the team to re-organize.

C. To explore ways to add more value to the customer.

D. To improve future iterations.

85. **Which of the following is not a value pair expressed in Agile Manifesto?**

A. Individuals and interactions over processes and tools.

B. Working software over comprehensive documentation.

C. Customer collaboration over meetings.

D. Responding to change over following a plan.

86. **In the Principles Behind the Agile Manifesto, what timeframe is expressed to deliver working software?**

A. One week.

B. A couple of days to a couple of weeks.

C. One month.

D. A couple of weeks to a couple of months.

87. **Units of work that do not necessarily add value but need to be done are known as:**

A. Capabilities.

B. Story points.

C. Work packages.

D. Tasks.

88. **Osmotic Communication describes**

A. The way team members overhear and absorb communication in their environment.

B. The set of tools and practices established to distribute communication to the team.

C. The information posted in the public area that the team and stakeholders can see.

D. One team member orally repeating relevant communication to the rest of the team to ensure it is distributed.

89. **If a team member is not performing up to team expectations, who should address this?**

A. The ScrumMaster.

B. The Team.

C. The Customer.

D. The person or group that recruited the team member.

90. **During early requirements-gathering, an important stakeholder repeatedly brings up concerns that are off-topic to the current requirements discussion. How should the team handle this?**
    A. The team should add the stakeholder's concerns to a parking lot chart.
    B. The team should call a break to allow the stakeholder to refocus.
    C. The team should ask the stakeholder to table any issues that are not related to the current discussion.
    D. The team should consider using a more concrete approach such as wireframes to provide a stronger point of focus for the stakeholder.

91. **Estimates of a user story used for estimating are known as:**
    A. Feature score.
    B. Fibonacci sequences.
    C. Story points.
    D. Planning poker.

92. **If a defect is detected on an Agile project, whose responsibility is it to correct the problem?**
    A. The person or pair that coded it.
    B. The Team's.
    C. The Product Owner's.
    D. The ScrumMaster's.

93. **A key difference between a work breakdown structure (WBS) and an Agile story map is:**
    A. A WBS is broken down, but a story map is not.
    B. A WBS is a two-dimensional model, but a story map is generally a three-dimensional model.
    C. A WBS should be complete, but a story map does not need to be.
    D. A WBS includes hammocks, but a story map includes hangers.

94. **Which statement is not true regarding user stories?**
    A. User stories should be aligned.
    B. User stories should be valuable.
    C. User stories should be small.
    D. User stories should be testable.

95. **George and Karen are working together on an Agile project. They have looked at the acceptance criteria and have built those into their modules first so that it must meet certain conditions to pass. George and Karen are practicing:**
    A.   Scrum.
    B.   eXtreme Programming.
    C.   Discrete Programming.
    D.   Test-Driven Development.

96. **Which statement below is true regarding the definition of "done"?**
    A.   It should be reconsidered after each iteration.
    B.   It should be agreed upon in advance by the entire team.
    C.   It changes for different modules.
    D.   It is a ground rule.

97. **Who is primarily responsible for creating the product roadmap?**
    A.   The Product Owner.
    B.   The Team.
    C.   The Project Manager.
    D.   The Stakeholders.

98. **The team is working on a group of user stories, but as they begin development they find they are unsure how to tell when the software works. How should the team manage this?**
    A.   The Team should get the software in the customer's hands and solicit feedback.
    B.   The Team is empowered to write acceptance criteria.
    C.   The Team should consult the test plan.
    D.   Ask the Customer to provide acceptance criteria before developing the user stories.

99. **When is the appropriate time to play Planning Poker?**
    A.   After the features have been requested but before the user stories have been written.
    B.   After the epics have been written but before the story map has been created.
    C.   After the user stories have been written but before the story points have been determined.
    D.   After the story points have been determined but before the acceptance tests have been created.

100. **In what way does Wideband Delphi differ from traditional Delphi?**

A.   The experts are aware of the other estimators in traditional Delphi.

B.   Wideband Delphi produces a range of estimates.

C.   Traditional Delphi produces a range of estimates.

D.   The experts are aware of the other estimators in Wideband Delphi.

PRACTICE TEST TWO

This second of two simulated PMI-ACP exam contains 100 questions.
Although the actual PMI-ACP exam contains 120 questions,
only 100 of these are scored and count toward your pass/fail grade.
Your target score is 82 correct or better. Your time limit is 2½ hours.

---

101. **A team member has communicated that she believes she can complete a user story in three days if there are no interruptions or distractions. This team member is:**
   A.   Timeboxing the user story.
   B.   Communicating in ideal time.
   C.   Not following Agile principles.
   D.   Disaggregating.

102. **Which practice listed below best reflects "continuous integration"?**
   A.   Checking in new features daily.
   B.   Getting software into the customer's hands frequently.
   C.   Frequent unit tests of all features.
   D.   Regularly reminding all team members of Agile practices.

103. **If an empowered team has drifted away from Agile practices, whose job is it to help them refocus?**
   A.   The coach.
   B.   The project management office (PMO).
   C.   The sponsor.
   D.   The team has to do this on its own.

104. **What primary role does the sponsor play on an Agile project?**
   A.   To provide product information and a product road map.
   B.   To approve a summary project plan.
   C.   To provide project funding and milestone-level goals.
   D.   To help define customer value.

---

105. On an Agile project, which of the following should happen over time?

A. Iterations should become shorter.

B. Velocity should remain the same.

C. Cycle times should become shorter.

D. Customer change-requests should become fewer.

106. A team runs firmly fixed 3-week iterations. Given the burn rate chart to the right, which statement is most likely true?

A. The team added members during iterations 4 and 5.

B. The team was less efficient during iterations 4 and 5.

C. The team was less productive during iterations 4 and 5.

D. The team was more productive during iterations 4 and 5.

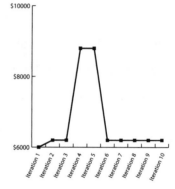

107. Who manages the iteration backlog?

A. The ScrumMaster.

B. The Product Owner.

C. The Sponsor.

D. The Team.

108. The Y-axis of a burn-up chart represents which of the following?

A. Resources.

B. Quality.

C. Functionality.

D. Time.

109. In Agile terminology, a "theme" is best described as:

A. The functional thrust behind a group of stories, an iteration, or a release.

B. The main business need driving or justifying the project.

C. An epic story.

D. The most prominent capability of the system.

110. The Product Roadmap:

A. Provides more information than the Charter but less than the Vision.

B. Is tailored to communicate with stakeholders.

C. It is most beneficial during requirements-gathering activities.

D. Provides more information than the Vision but less information than User Stories.

111. **Which of the following meetings would a Product Owner most likely not be invited to?**
   A.   Iteration retrospective.
   B.   Release planning meeting.
   C.   Daily stand-up meeting.
   D.   Iteration planning meeting.

112. **Which of the following best represents Scrum values?**
   A.   Collection, Introspection, Adaptation.
   B.   Communication, Coordination, Adaptation.
   C.   Realism, Sustainability, Adaptation.
   D.   Visibility, Inspection, Adaptation.

113. **The team has released a build that is not in compliance with their organization's coding standards. Which statement below is true?**
   A.   This contributes to technical debt.
   B.   This represents a violation of the ground rules.
   C.   This is outside of the definition of "done."
   D.   This is acceptable as long as value is delivered to the customer.

114. **During planning poker, the Team provides estimates in:**
   A.   Days.
   B.   Hours.
   C.   Story Points.
   D.   Dollars.

115. **The smallest set of functionality that has value to the customer is:**
   A.   A story point.
   B.   A minimal marketable feature.
   C.   A user story.
   D.   A function.

116. **A Sprint has ended. What comes next?**
   A.   The release.
   B.   The retrospective.
   C.   The next Sprint.
   D.   The Scrum of Scrums.

117. **A project stakeholder has asked for a current status on the project. What is the best way to address this request?**
     A.   The Coach should gather statuses at the daily stand-up and provide them
     B.   Ask the Product Owner to provide the information to the stakeholder.
     C.   Hold a status meeting with the stakeholder and the Team.
     D.   Direct the stakeholder to the information radiator.

118. **The Team has just begun Iteration H. Which of the following would be expected during this iteration?**
     A.   No new functionality is being developed.
     B.   The Team is primarily engaged in planning and estimating.
     C.   The Team is demonstrating the product.
     D.   The Team considering process improvement.

119. **A program has been broken down into multiple Agile projects. The project management organization (PMO) has asked that the various teams coordinate. What is the best way to accomplish this?**
     A.   Agile tooling.
     B.   Colocate all teams.
     C.   Initiate Scrum of Scrums meetings.
     D.   Aggregate information radiators.

120. **On a Scrum project, The single voice of the user is represented by:**
     A.   The ScrumMaster.
     B.   The Product Owner.
     C.   The Team.
     D.   The Sponsor.

121. **The team is halfway through an iteration when the customer asks to introduce new functionality into the iteration backlog. What is the most appropriate response by the team, and why?**
     A.   Allow this, since Agile welcomes changing requirements.
     B.   Allow this, since the customer has the final say.
     C.   Oppose this since the iteration backlog is fixed.
     D.   Ask the ScrumMaster or Coach to decide since he or she has the final say.

122. **If your team is not ready to apply all of the XP practices, they should try to apply which of the following?**
 A. The first 6.
 B. The first 10.
 C. The first 12.
 D. XP will not work well unless all of the practices are applied.

123. **Grooming takes place at which level?**
 A. Iteration backlog.
 B. Task.
 C. Product backlog.
 D. Personal.

124. **Given the iteration burn-down chart to the right with the upper slanted line representing planned progress and the lighter, jagged line below representing actual progress and the vertical dashed line representing the current day, which statement below is accurate?**

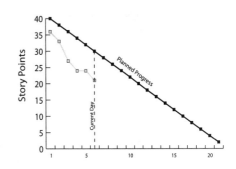

 A. The team is at risk of finishing the iteration ahead of schedule.
 B. The team is at risk of finishing the iteration behind schedule.
 C. The team is at risk of finishing the iteration under budget.
 D. The team is at risk of finishing the iteration over budget.

125. **In a product backlog, where would you expect to find epic stories?**
 A. In the disaggregation pool.
 B. Epic stories should not appear in the product backlog.
 C. At or near the top.
 D. At or near the bottom.

126. **Which of the following is not a Scrum ceremony?**
 A. Sprint planning.
 B. Daily stand-up.
 C. Sprint.
 D. Sprint retrospective.

127. **A primary difference between Agile and traditional management is:**

    A.   Agile favors adaptation, while traditional methods favor anticipation.

    B.   Agile favors consensus, while traditional methods favor plan-do-check-act.

    C.   Agile favors the product, while traditional methods favor the process.

    D.   Agile favors the team, while traditional methods favor the organization.

128. **Which of the following statements about the product backlog is correct?**

    A.   Each user story in the product backlog must be disaggregated and have user acceptance criteria.

    B.   The user stories should be the responsibility of the team.

    C.   The user stories should be the responsibility of the Coach or ScrumMaster.

    D.   The user stories at the bottom may not be as well defined as the ones at the top.

129. **The Team is starting an iteration planning meeting, and the Product Owner is not present. Is this a problem?**

    A.   Yes. As a Team member the product owner is required to be present for all team meetings.

    B.   No. The Team is self-organizing and should be able to resolve any questions on its own.

    C.   No. The Product Owner is not supposed to be involved in the iteration planning meeting.

    D.   Yes. The Product Owner spends part of the iteration planning meeting explaining the user stories to the team.

130. **A new Team member wants to know what the most important undeveloped user story is. What is the best way for her to proceed?**

    A.   Look at the bottom of the product backlog.

    B.   Look at the top of the product backlog.

    C.   Look at the burn down chart.

    D.   Ask the Team.

131. **You are introducing Agile principles to an organization. A senior manager has asked about the importance of planning under Agile. Which statement below would be the most helpful in explaining this?**

    A.   Agile projects value customer collaboration over following a plan.

    B.   Agile projects favor planning closer in time to the actual event.

    C.   Agile projects plan much less than traditional projects.

    D.   Agile projects do not value planning.

132. **The team is having a strong disagreement about whether to build or buy a component. What is the best way to proceed?**
  A.   Ask the Coach or ScrumMaster for direction.
  B.   As the product owner for direction.
  C.   Wait for consensus.
  D.   Create a spike to help answer the question.

133. **A Product Owner wishes to introduce a change in the middle of an iteration. The change would extend the iteration by one week. How should the team respond?**
  A.   Encourage the product owner to wait until the next iteration.
  B.   Embrace the change.
  C.   Ask the Coach or ScrumMaster for direction.
  D.   Inform the product owner of the consequences and allow him or her to make the decision.

134. **Who writes user stories?**
  A.   The Team.
  B.   The Customer.
  C.   The Users.
  D.   The Testers.

135. **How long should daily stand-up meetings be?**
  A.   No more than 15 minutes.
  B.   No more than 5 minutes.
  C.   No more than 30 minutes.
  D.   As long as the Team determines that value is being added.

136. **Which statement below about the release plan is accurate?**
  A.   The release plan represents a commitment made by the team.
  B.   A single iteration could contain more than one release.
  C.   The release plan is generally driven by the Coach or ScrumMaster.
  D.   The release plan may be fluid, depending on the team's velocity.

137. **"Decide as late as possible" is most closely associated with which methodology?**
  A.   XP.
  B.   Scrum.
  C.   Lean.
  D.   Kanban.

138. Which statement below regarding cost estimating is accurate?

A. Costs are generally estimated when the product backlog is populated.

B. Costs are expected to drop as iterations progress.

C. Costs are estimated as a function of the burn rate, velocity, product backlog, and release plan.

D. Because iterations are very short, costs are not estimated up front but are calculated at the end of each iteration.

139. What should a Coach's attitude toward conflict be?

A. Some team conflict can be healthy.

B. Conflict should be ignored unless it affects value.

C. Because team is valued, conflict should always be avoided.

D. Because team is valued, conflict should always end in consensus.

140. Which basis of comparison listed below is most meaningful on an Agile project?

A. Velocities between two teams.

B. Return on investment between two teams.

C. Cycle times between two teams.

D. Story points completed between two teams.

141. On an Agile project, how is the schedule built?

A. By estimating story points and applying velocity.

B. Through decomposition and estimation of tasks.

C. By analyzing tasks and determining dependencies.

D. Agile iterations are timeboxed, so the schedule is essentially predetermined.

142. What is the primary means an Agile team uses to communicate with outside stakeholders?

A. The project management plan.

B. The communication management plan.

C. Face to face meetings.

D. The information radiator.

143. If an Agile project is release-timeboxed, which of the following statements is true?

A. The releases are not flexible with schedule, but the iteratations are.

B. Planning time is fixed.

C. The overall schedule is predetermined.

D. The team has less overall flexibility.

144. **How often should the entire Team meet on an Agile project?**
    A.   Daily.
    B.   Weekly.
    C.   It depends upon the length of the iteration.
    D.   As often as the Team agrees is necessary.

145. **An Agile team has collective responsibility for everything except for:**
    A.   The code.
    B.   The product backlog.
    C.   The quality of the product.
    D.   The speed at which stories are completed.

146. **For the past week, the Customer has been using the stand-up meeting to discuss errors he has been detecting in the product. Which response would be appropriate?**
    A.   The Team should explain that this is an inappropriate use of a daily stand-up.
    B.   The Sponsor should be involved to resolve the situation.
    C.   The Team should listen to the Customer since this represents an obstacle.
    D.   The ScrumMaster should explain the purpose of the daily stand-up meeting to the Customer.

147. **In which of the following environments would an Agile project be the best fit?**
    A.   A complex project where the requirements are mostly undetermined.
    B.   A complex project where the requirements are firmly set.
    C.   A simple project where the requirements are mostly undetermined.
    D.   A simple project where the requirements are firmly set.

148. **Which statement below concerning the risk-adjusted backlog is most accurate?**
    A.   The risk-adjusted backlog is based on qualitative risks.
    B.   The risk-adjusted backlog is based on quantitative risks.
    C.   The risk-adjusted backlog will be ordered differently than the product backlog.
    D.   The risk-adjusted backlog shows risk events that have already occurred and risk events that may occur in the future.

149. **All of the following are Lean principles except:**
    A.   Test as early as possible.
    B.   See the whole.
    C.   Decide as late as possible.
    D.   Build integrity in.

150. **Which statement is false about risk?**
- A. Risks are any uncertain event, positive or negative.
- B. Risks may be represented on a risk-adjusted backlog.
- C. Risks must be quantified to be understood.
- D. Value should be evaluated against risk.

151. **Which of the following is not a part of active listening?**
- A. Listening.
- B. Understanding.
- C. Retaining.
- D. Recording.

152. **An Agile team is playing an innovation game. What is the most likely purpose of this?**
- A. To improve the overall process.
- B. To look for new ways to deliver value to the customer.
- C. To gather requirements.
- D. To understand the underlying factors that cause change.

153. **Which management style is most closely associated with Agile?**
- A. Participatory.
- B. Team.
- C. None.
- D. Adaptive.

154. **What is the goal of the planning game?**
- A. To maximize value.
- B. To engage the customer.
- C. To capture user stories that might otherwise be missed.
- D. To accurately document the iteration's scope.

155. **The team has created fictitious identities to imagine how this user might interact with the system. What is the team doing?**
- A. Playing an innovation game.
- B. Playing a planning game.
- C. Creating personas.
- D. Imagineering.

156. Tasks are defined:
    A.   At the point that user stories are written.
    B.   During iteration planning.
    C.   During release planning.
    D.   After the daily stand-ups.

157. Who is responsible for ensuring that the project's return on investment (ROI) meets its projections?
    A.   The ScrumMaster.
    B.   The Team.
    C.   The Tracker.
    D.   The Product Owner.

158. Which of the following choices represents the best description of technical debt?
    A.   The accumulated cost of bringing a resource on the team who is unfamiliar with Agile.
    B.   The accumulated cost of postponing a necessary technical decision or implementation.
    C.   The accumulated cost of implementing a new technology.
    D.   The accumulated cost of replacing a manual process or practice with a technical solution.

159. A Coach has reminded her team to "be DRY today." What was she encouraging them to do?
    A.   Not to release code too early.
    B.   To regressing test all new work prior to checking it in.
    C.   Not to redo something that has already been done.
    D.   To document their code.

160. The team is estimating the effort associated with user stories. How will this be represented?
    A.   Tasks.
    B.   Cycle time.
    C.   Ideal days.
    D.   Velocity.

161. **If there is a disagreement over the order of the iteration backlog, who should resolve it?**

    A.   The Coach.

    B.   The Product Owner.

    C.   The Tracker.

    D.   The Team.

162. **Which of the following is most closely associated with the waterfall approach?**

    A.   Systems Development Life Cycle.

    B.   Product Life Cycle.

    C.   Project management.

    D.   Deming's Cycle.

163. **Which Agile methodology explicitly encourages the use of metaphor?**

    A.   Scrum

    B.   Kanban

    C.   XP

    D.   Lean

164. **The team has installed a new version control package to help with daily builds. This is an example of:**

    A.   Technical debt.

    B.   Agile tooling.

    C.   Integrated technology.

    D.   Agile Configuration Management.

165. **The main focus of an Agile Coach should be:**

    A.   To help the team follow the twelve XP processes.

    B.   To maximize customer value.

    C.   To maximize the work not done.

    D.   To direct and manage project execution.

166. **Which statement below is true concerning the payback period calculation?**

    A.   Risk should be factored in before the calculation is performed.

    B.   Payback period should not be used by itself to make a determination.

    C.   It is only useful when compared to other projects in the same organization.

    D.   A smaller number is more desirable than a larger one.

167. **How are burn-down charts used?**
   A.   Burn-down charts are used to calculate cycle time.
   B.   Burn-down charts are a primary tool of risk management.
   C.   Burn-down charts depict a form of scope and schedule progress.
   D.   Burn-down charts depict a form of cost and schedule progress.

168. **Actual time and ideal time differ because of:**
   A.   Interruptions.
   B.   Miscalculations.
   C.   Responding to change.
   D.   The coefficient of team friction.

169. **The number of stories a team can deliver in an iteration is known as:**
   A.   Velocity.
   B.   Cycle time.
   C.   Burn rate.
   D.   Capacity.

170. **Product risk is primarily the responsibility of:**
   A.   The ScrumMaster.
   B.   The Product Owner.
   C.   The Team.
   D.   The Project Management Office (PMO).

171. **How is an Agile project's schedule generally established?**
   A.   Through a calculation of work packages and effort.
   B.   Through a calculation of tasks, dependencies, and durations.
   C.   By determining the critical path.
   D.   Through a calculation of story points and team velocity.

172. **A stakeholder who is only loosely involved in the project has asked the ScrumMaster if she may begin attending the team's daily stand-up meetings. How should the ScrumMaster respond?**
   A.   Invite the stakeholder to attend and participate in the meeting.
   B.   Invite the stakeholder to attend but not participate in the meeting.
   C.   Invite the stakeholder to the Sprint retrospective instead.
   D.   Have the Team to vote on the request.

173. **A team's release burn-down chart shows an upward spike between the third and fourth iterations. What could account for this?**

A. The team's cycle time dropped.

B. The team's velocity dropped.

C. User stories were added to the release backlog.

D. The team's burn rate increased.

174. **A project team has a velocity of 16. Given the product backlog represented in the table below, what is the best combination of iterations?**

User Story	Priority	Estimate
A	1	4
B	2	3
C	3	9
D	4	1 3
E	5	3
F	6	1 5
G	7	3
H	8	2
I	9	1
J	1 0	3
K	1 1	5
L	1 2	5

A. Iteration 1: ABC; Iteration 2: DE; Iteration 3: FG; Iteration 4: HIJKL.

B. Iteration 1: ABC; Iteration 2: DE; Iteration 3: FI; Iteration 4: GHJK; Iteration 5: L.

C. Iteration 1: ABC; Iteration 2: DE; Iteration 3: GHIJK; Iteration 4: F; Iteration 5:L.

D. Iteration 1: ABC; Iteration 2: DE; Iteration 3: GHIKL; Iteration 5: F.

175. **The definition of "done" is:**

A. Best taken from the Principles Behind the Agile Manifesto.

B. Best determined by the team.

C. Best determined by the customer.

D. Best if it incorporates customer acceptance.

176. The term Kanban most closely means:

    A.   Signal.

    B.   Continuous improvement.

    C.   Process.

    D.   Workflow.

177. An iteration has ended. You are the coach of a team that has developed a feature for this iteration, but your customer says it does not meet his acceptance criteria. How should you respond?

    A.   Perform a spike to determine whether there is quick fix available to make the feature acceptable.

    B.   Add it to the next iteration backlog.

    C.   Bring this up at the next daily stand-up and perform root cause analysis.

    D.   Improve your implementation of test-first development.

178. On a Scrum project, how often are team efforts coordinated?

    A.   Daily.

    B.   Weekly.

    C.   Monthly.

    D.   The team determines this.

179. A team's velocity has been slowly and unexpectedly falling throughout the project. Is this a concern?

    A.   Not if the cycle time improves by a corresponding amount.

    B.   Not if it does not impede delivery of customer value.

    C.   Yes, it will affect the team's burn rate, all other things being equal.

    D.   Yes, it should be improving over time, all other things being equal.

180. A Kanban board is used for all of the following except:

    A.   To help limit WIP.

    B.   To contribute to the information radiator.

    C.   To help visualize workflow.

    D.   To help visualize the product backlog.

181. Which document would be the most important on an Agile project?

    A.   The Schedule Management Plan.

    B.   The Cost Management Plan.

    C.   The Work Breakdown Structure.

    D.   The Charter.

182. Senior management has indicated to the ScrumMaster that colocation of a particular Agile team is impossible. What is the best response?

    A.   Insist that team be colocated.

    B.   Invest in software that helps create a live presence.

    C.   Consider switching the project to waterfall methodology.

    D.   No action is needed.

183. The Product Vision Statement contains all of the following attributes except:

    A.   What the product is.

    B.   Why it is needed.

    C.   Why Agile is the right approach for this project.

    D.   Why someone would pay for it.

184. The document that shows planned releases and relevant features is:

    A.   The Product Roadmap.

    B.   The Agile Release Plan.

    C.   The Project Management Plan.

    D.   The Iteration Plan.

185. Which acronym below describes the product backlog?

    A.   INVEST.

    B.   SURE.

    C.   GROOM.

    D.   DEEP.

186. The team is meeting to discuss estimates. For each estimate, the range is plotted on a graph to be discussed. Which method is this team using?

    A.   Affinity Estimating.

    B.   Hi-Low Estimating.

    C.   Wideband Delphi.

    D.   Fibonacci Number Sequencing.

187. All other things being equal, which estimating technique is the fastest?

    A.   Planning Poker.

    B.   Affinity Estimating.

    C.   Wideband Delphi.

    D.   Scatter.

188. In Leas' Conflict Model, level one represents

  A. A problem to solve.

  B. A disagreement.

  C. A contest.

  D. A world war.

189. Which statement below is true regarding Earned Value Management (EVM) on Agile?

  A. EVM is generally less accurate on Agile projects since the scope is not fully defined.

  B. EVM is generally more difficult to calculate on Agile projects due to the way progress is tracked.

  C. EVM is affected by the cone of uncertainty.

  D. EVM is no different for Agile projects since the underlying calculations remain the same.

190. You have just begun working on an Agile project as a new team member. On the wall is a chart that shows items that are backlogged, started, designed, coded, and done. What kind of chart is this?

  A. Burn-down chart.

  B. Cumulative Flow Diagram.

  C. Burn-up chart.

  D. Ishikawa Diagram.

191. Which methodology makes it a point to amplify learning?

  A. XP.

  B. Scrum.

  C. Lean.

  D. Kanban.

192. In which project environments would Agile best be applied?

  A. In chaotic environments.

  B. In environments where relatively complex decision making is necessary.

  C. In environments where things are relatively close to agreement and close to certainty.

  D. In environments where things are relatively far from agreement and far from certainty.

193. The opposite of an information radiator is:

  A. An information broker.

  B. An information vacuum.

  C. An information consolidator.

  D. An information refrigerator.

194. **The best tool for representing the work remaining for a project is:**
   A. The iteration backlog.
   B. The product backlog.
   C. The velocity graph.
   D. The iteration burn-down chart.

195. **Which methodology tries to remove project uncertainty?**
   A. XP.
   B. Scrum.
   C. Kanban.
   D. Waterfall.

196. **You are working on an Agile Team when a stakeholder drops by to ask how the current iteration is progressing. Where would you direct her?**
   A. To the Product Owner.
   B. To the ScrumMaster.
   C. To the iteration burn-down chart.
   D. To the release plan.

197. **Who are the best people to recruit onto an Agile team?**
   A. Individuals who are generalists.
   B. Individuals who are specialists
   C. Individuals who are self-directing.
   D. Individuals who avoid conflict.

198. **When would you most likely expect to see recently-developed functionality demonstrated by the team?**
   A. At the iteration retrospective.
   B. At the Scrum or Scrums.
   C. At the release party.
   D. At the iteration review.

199. **A customer asks who will be developing a specific feature in this iteration. How should you direct the customer?**
   A. Look at the iteration backlog.
   B. Look at the release backlog.
   C. Explain that the team is collectively responsible for all features.
   D. Attend the daily stand-up meeting.

200. On an Agile project, how would you expect to see risk managed?

    A.   By following the risk management plan (RMP).

    B.   By ordering stories in the risk-adjusted backlog.

    C.   By evaluating risk in the risk assessment matrix (RAM).

    D.   By creating a risk tree.

ANSWERS TO
PRACTICE TEST ONE

1. **B.** Principle #2 in The Principles Behind the Agile Manifesto states "[we] welcome changing requirements, even late in development. Agile processes harness change for the Customer's competitive advantage." Answer 'A' really doesn't work well. If you embrace change, you will likely receive more change requests. 'C' is not a good choice since self-organizing teams can likely adapt better than traditional teams, but it would not be instant. 'D' is not correct since Kaizen stands for continuous improvement, which is not necessarily strongly aligned to change.

2. **C.** Scrum specifies that the iteration planning meeting (held at the beginning of each iteration) should last no longer than eight hours.

3. **C.** Refactoring simply reorganizes the code to make it more logical and maintainable by the team. It does not affect efficiency or effectiveness. Answer 'B' could be correct (i.e., it may well be done), but that would vary depending on the team's definition of "done," leaving 'C' as the best answer.

4. **A.** The Team member needs to communicate this. It is an obstacle that should be brought up in the daily stand-up meetings. 'B' would not be the right role if the Team member were to escalate this. 'C' is close to being correct, but Team members bring up obstacles to the entire Team, and the ScrumMaster then works to eliminate them.

5. **B.** Reading the glossary (more than once) will pay big dividends on the exam. Face-to-face communication is a form of high-bandwidth communication.

6.   **D.** Story points are assigned to the iteration backlog. They are applied to each user story (if user story had been a choice here, it would have been the best choice).

7.   **B.** Present Value calculates current value without considering costs, while Net Present Value does the same thing but subtracts costs out at the end.

8.   **A.** Each other answer is true; however, the charter is just as applicable to Agile projects as it is to traditional ones. Regardless of the methodology, projects that bypass the chartering process run a higher risk of cancellation and other problems than those that do have a charter.

9.   **D.** The ScrumMaster's primary role is to help the team stay focused on Agile principles. 'A' is the worst choice of the four, as the ScrumMaster does not manage the team or the project. 'B' is incorrect since the product owner would likely fill this role. 'C' is not a bad answer, as the ScrumMaster could, perhaps, be asked to measure and report progress to senior management; however, it is not always the case, and it is not the best answer of the four.

10. **C.** The Scrum Guide, by Agile co-creators Schwaber and Sutherland indicates that the optimal size is 7 team members ± 2, which translates to 5 to 9.

11. **B.** Ground rules are not written by the ScrumMaster. They are rules that apply to all team member, and they are often informal. 'A', 'C', and 'D' all apply to ground rules (this question asked which was false).

12. **C.** A stakeholder is anyone with an interest in the project. 'A' and 'D' could work under certain circumstances. 'B' describes into the difference between "pigs" and "chickens" (see glossary) but a stakeholder encompasses both of these. 'C' is closest to the actual definition, making it the best answer.

13. **A.** There are several "innovation games" covered in Chapter 6. This one is a game called "Buy a Feature". You should know the different games presented in that section before sitting for the exam.

14. **C.** Force field analysis looks at the factors for and against change and assigns a number to them to understand the aggregate force on each side. 'A' is not a good choice, since root cause analysis is not a numerical analysis like the question described. 'B' occurs early in the project and does not do numerical analysis either, and 'D' is a made-up term.

15. **B.** The best technique here would be to create personas. These personas are used to elicit requirements by imagining how fictional users would interact with the product or system. 'A' is not a bad answer, but it doesn't solve the problem the way personas would. 'C' does not work well for this situation, since you have to have a problem to analyze to do root cause analysis, and no problem is presented here. 'D' is another "almost" answer, but it isn't the best answer since wireframes might be something you create after you understand how users will use your system, and you really aren't to that point yet.

16. **A.** An epic story is a large story that may span iterations. It is also known as a capability.

17. **B.** Test-first development is implemented by writing the test cases first and designing the modules, classes, and functions around these tests. Software is written in the context of how it will be accepted. When this is done correctly, the software should be acceptable when it passes the tests around which it is constructed.

18. **C.** Relative sizing is the practice of estimating something as requiring more effort or less effort than something else. 'A' is a different technique using the Fibonacci number sequence, 0, 1, 2, 3, 5, 8, 13... It does not fit the description here well. 'B' is not a good answer since the team is placing things on the wall, and in planning poker the team generally uses playing cards. 'D' is not a good answer since affinity estimating generally uses coffee cup sizes or shirt sizes or some other measure that the team can relate back to their effort.

19. **B.** One of the key tenets of Agile is that software is collectively maintained, and the team is responsible for all of it. The scenario in the question makes Jerry the only one who can maintain it, and this is a problem for everyone involved. 'A' is not necessarily correct. Some teams may have this rule, and some may not. 'C' is also a rule that may vary from team to team, depending on the definition of done. 'D' is not the best answer, since not all conflict has to be dealt with immediately. The bigger problem is not that there is conflict but that Jerry is operating in his own silo, and the team is not working as a team.

20. **C.** This is a classic example of affinity estimating where the team compares their effort to something else they can relate to. Common usages include shirt sizes or coffee cup sizes.

21. **A.** A wireframe is a quick way to mock up a screen without any real functionality or code. It's a fast way to show the users a concept that they can understand. 'B' is a description of a prototype and not a wireframe, since wireframes do not function. 'C' is not good, since a wireframe is not a substitute for documentation. 'D' is not a good choice, since the point of a wireframe is to let the user see it and not to streamline the interface.

22. **D.** Timeboxing is a means of managing a project where the time is firmly established. Only the features that have been accepted when the time limit is reached are included. 'A' is not a good answer, since timeboxing still uses iterations just like other methods. 'B' is accurate, but the question asks for the false statement. 'C' is also accurate (remember, the question asks for the false statement) because timeboxing can cause the team to shift their focus from Customer value to what can be accomplished technically.

23. **C.** Ed Deming is credited with documenting and popularizing the now-famous plan-do-check-

act cycle.

24. **B.** The idea is that working software is favored over comprehensive documentation, and the desired level of documentation is often described as "barely sufficient" on Agile projects. 'A' is completely unrealistic. 'C' does not capture the spirit of Agile, since the word "thorough" is too close to "comprehensive." 'D' is what you would want on a traditional project or if the team were siloed, but since Agile teams are all in the same space, this kind of documentation is likely overkill.

25. **A.** The closest match to continuous integration is that code should be checked in and tested each day. This was a tricky question, since this is a very imperfect answer, but it was the best choice. Continuous integration may mean that changes are checked in each hour (not necessarily each day). 'B' is incorrect, since each team member could have a local copy of the code, creating multiple temporary codebases. 'C' is not a good answer since the Customer would neither want nor benefit from receiving code in real time. 'D' is not a bad guess, but the words "feature complete" do not appear in this book (one clue that it was not a good answer), and this depends on the definition of done.

26. **B.** Make sure you understand a minimal marketable feature (MMF) before sitting for the exam. It is the smallest bit of functionality that adds value to the Customer or use, and it is desirable on Agile projects, since it provides a good-sized unit for the team to work with. 'A' is not a good answer, since a story point is something the team uses to estimate, but it has no value to the Customer. 'C' would be a breakdown of a larger user story, but it is not a solid choice for this question. 'D' is not a good choice since use cases show how users will interact, but they are not necessarily small, and they do not necessarily add value.

27. **A.** An iteration in generic Agile is the same as a Sprint in the methodology, Scrum. 'B' and 'C' do not fit well since they are about speed and an iteration is closer to a duration. 'D' is not a good choice, since a release may have many iterations.

28. **B.** XP is firm that a pair of developers may not commit to more story points than they were able to complete in the previous iteration. The question asked which statement was false, making 'B' the best choice. 'A' is not a good choice, since XP does pair programmers. 'C' is not a good choice since the iterations are shorter than other methodologies (usually one week) in XP. 'D' is also true about XP (and the question asked for the false statement).

29. **B.** Earned Value Management (EVM) is captured and communicated at the iteration level.

30. **D.** The fact that it is XP is not particularly important in answering this question. The answer would be the same regardless of the methodology. It is the Coach's job to keep the team focused on Agile principles and to remove obstacles. In this case, the stakeholder is an obstacle through the distractions. The Coach should take the person aside and explain how focus and

the need for a distraction-free environment are so important. 'A' is the worst answer here. Not everyone needs to be on the team. 'B' is closer, but this is the Coach's job and not the team's job. 'C' is not a good answer since it is the Coach's responsibility.

31. **B.** The defined roles on the XP project are Coach, Customer, Programmer, Tester, and Tracker.

32. **B.** Iterations are smaller than releases, so a release may (and probably does) contain multiple iterations, but an iteration cannot contain multiple releases. 'A', 'C', and 'D' are all correct statements, and the question asked for the one that is false.

33. **D.** Value Stream Mapping looks at a series of processes and follows them through the entire system to understand them better and analyze the value they deliver. 'C' is not a good match, since a Cumulative Flow Diagram shows workflow of tasks but not of processes. 'A' and 'B' were made-up terms.

34. **D.** You cannot compare the velocity of one team to another for the simple reason that velocity is based on story points, and the meaning of a story point can and will vary widely among teams. The best choice is to explain this to senior management. 'A' assumes that one team is performing better than the other, but that is not evident here. 'B' is not a particularly bad answer except that senior management did not ask for that, and they may not know what to do with the earned value measurements you collect. 'C' also assumes that there is a problem to be solved, but there may not be.

35. **A.** Lean is fanatical about reducing waste. One of the ways it accomplishes this is by seeking to maximize the work that is not done.

36. **C.** The capitalized words are one clue that we are talking about Scrum, but you should have answered it correctly even if you did not pick up on that. The Product Owner is primarily responsible for creating, updating, and grooming the product backlog.

37. **C.** While some Agile theorists might bristle at this, Agile is generally considered to be very challenging to scale to large teams. 'A', 'B', and 'D' are all very Agile (the question asked for the one that is least Agile).

38. **D.** The team is responsible for tracking its own progress. Kanban boards show status, and no one knows the status of an item better than team member doing the work. If the choice had been there for "The Tracker" (a role in XP), that would have been a better choice, but it was not present.

39. **D.** This requires a relatively deep understanding of what these charts are and how they are used. 'A' is not correct because neither chart shows the addition of new user stories particularly well. This would be something the backlog would show. 'B' is not a good choice both a burn-down chart and a cumulative flow diagram will show the addition of new user stories clearly. 'C' is not a good choice since they are updated as needed during an iteration. This leaves 'D' as the best

answer since a cumulative flow diagram shows work as it progresses through the system, so work that has been begun but not finished is shown. A burn-down chart does not show work until it is done, so this would be one key area they differ.

40. **B.** Scrum has the majority of the market share and is the most popular Agile methodology in use at this time. See Chapter 9 for the breakdown and percentages.

41. **C.** This is the definition of cycle time. 'A' represents the number of story points a team can complete in an iteration. 'B' is not a term from this book (nor is it particularly Agile), and 'D' represents the cost of the team per iteration.

42. **A.** The number of story points the team can complete in an iteration is known as the team's velocity.

43. **D.** The burn rate reflects the labor costs for a given iteration and could be used to calculate future iterations.

44. **D.** Escaped defects are those errors that the Customer finds. If they are detected by the team before they get to the Customer, they are not escaped defects. 'A', 'B', and 'C' could be correct to varying levels, but the question is the very definition of an escaped defect.

45. **B.** Kaizen is the Japanese philosophy of continuous improvement, which is carried out through small changes. 'A' is the translation for another Japanese management term (Kanban). 'C' and 'D' are both Agile concepts, but they do not reflect the philosophy of Kaizen.

46. **A.** The right order for Test-driven development is test, code, refactor, deliver. If it seems impossible to test before you code, consider that you are creating the test cases and building them into the module before you write it. The module is then written to pass the tests. After that it is refactored and delivered to the Customer.

47. **A.** A spike (also called a spike solution) is a small experiment used to determine a course of action when there is a question about how to proceed.

48. **C.** In Iteration Zero, the team generally plans, and no working software is delivered to the Customer. Remember that in Agile, a plan does not hold intrinsic value. It is working software that conveys value.

49. **D.** Limiting WIP is most closely associated with Kanban. The Kanban board shows work progressing through the system, and it is used to limit WIP and help the team to maintain focus on a very few items.

50. **C.** The Product Owner or Customer is the final arbitrator of the value functionality does or does not provide.

51. **A.** The Agile Coach is employing emotional intelligence. The key here is that the Coach is trying

to understand the other's concerns and to relate. While 'A' is not a perfect fit for this question, it is the best of the four. 'B' does not work since there is no evidence of "active" listening (e.g., giving feedback, ensuring understanding). 'C' does not fit since there is no evidence of collaboration taking place. 'D' is the next best answer, but it is not a term used in this book, and the negotiation taking place is different than conflict resolution.

52. **B.** An organization that embraces Agile should expect more change requests, since Agile welcomes changing requirements, even if they are introduced late in the project.

53. **C.** Remember the INVEST acronym (you need to know it before sitting for the exam)! User stories should be (I)ndependent, (N)egotiable, (V)aluable, (E)stimable, (S)mall, and (T)estable.

54. **B.** Principle seven in The Principles Behind the Agile Manifesto states that "Working software is the primary measure of progress." All other things may indicate progress, but nothing speaks louder than results, and results are expressed through working software on Agile products.

55. **D.** eXtreme Programming (XP) projects have programmers work in pairs.

56. **A.** The Product Owner is the person who lays out which user stories are the highest priority and provides functional specifics on those features or user stories. This takes place as part of the iteration planning meeting.

57. **D.** You needed to read this one carefully. Tasks are not assigned. The team takes them on and self-organizes around them. They are agreed upon, but not assigned. 'A' is accurate (the question wanted the false statement) in that they do not necessarily add Customer value by themselves. 'B' is not a good choice, since tasks do represent the smallest breakdown of work. 'C' is not a good choice, because tasks may show up on a Kanban board or other form of information radiator.

58. **B** Sprint review or retrospective is one half-day (four hours).

59. **C.** Agile teams escalate fewer issues than waterfall teams because Agile teams are empowered to resolve issues, and because the Customer or product owner is likely colocated with them, so there is no need to escalate issues. Instead, most issues are rapidly resolved on the spot.

60. **B.** Continuous improvement, while a very Agile concept, is not mentioned in the Agile Manifesto.

61. **A.** Daily stand-up meetings allow the team to coordinate work and communicate issues with each other by sharing information out in the open. 'B' and 'C' are great byproducts of the meetings, but they are not their primary purpose. 'D' is more descriptive of the retrospective or

review meetings than the daily stand-ups.

62. **A.** Understanding the roles is very important! Product Owners need to help prioritize the product backlog, serve as the single voice of the Customer, and accept the work. 'B' is incorrect because they do not prioritize the iteration backlog (the team manages this), and they do not coordinate team activities. They do communicate the value of user stories to the team, however. 'C' is incorrect since they certainly do not facilitate daily stand-ups (the team does this itself). They do write user stories. 'D' is incorrect since Teams don't get outside help from Product Owners in self-organization.

63. **C.** When any component is not complete at the end of an iteration, it should be identified and restored to the Product Backlog as incomplete work. 'A' is a very poor choice for this scenario. 'B' is incorrect since it would be the Product Owner's or the Customer's decision and not the Coach's. 'D' might sound good if you don't understand how an iteration works, but once the time limit is up, the iteration ends.

64. **B.** Distributed teams may be a reality, but they are not ideal. Under Agile, distributed teams will probably be less effective than colocated teams.

65. **A.** Principle five in the Principles Behind the Agile Manifesto states that we should "build projects around motivated individuals." 'B' and 'D' are not very Agile choices. C is not a good choice, since Agile projects are both about the process and the product.

66. **A.** Escaped defects are a problem, and the team has to be brought into this situation and made aware. 'B' is not good since the entire team is collectively responsible for the results. 'C' might be a good step, but it probably isn't sufficient by itself. 'D' would be insufficient since the team might not address this situation for quite some time if it waited until the next iteration retrospective.

67. **B.** Agile teams do not produce "detailed project plans," so it would be best to educate senior management that rather than doing this, the team will be delivering working, valuable software. 'A' is not what senior management asked for, so this is not a good response. 'C' does not work well since they may not have these components, and developing abbreviated versions would not make sense. 'D' is not a good choice for this scenario since it is not what senior management requested, and it likely would not be well received.

68. **C.** An Agile team's workflow is agreed upon by the team. For example, it may be that tasks are "Started, Designed, Coded, Tested, Done," or they may create a different workflow entirely. The point is that it is defined by and belongs to the team. 'A' is not a good choice, since that looks like the command and control model that Agile seeks to avoid. 'B' is incorrect since user stories are in the backlog, but the workflow is not. 'D' is not a good choice, because while the workflow would certainly contribute to quality, it is by no means the primary contributor.

69. **A.** The key to understanding this is to look at the velocity. By keeping it at 5, the combination of AB for iteration 1, CDE for iteration 2, and F for iteration 3 works perfectly. There is no need to rearrange the priorities or change the length of any iterations in this case.

70. **D.** The wording on this question and the corresponding answer is tricky. Agile smells are issues that might appear as something else on the surface. For example, if the coach has begun assigning work to the team, that might be classified as a "smell." The underlying problem might be that self-organization has broken down.

71. **A.** Prune the Product Tree is an innovation game used in requirements gathering.

72. **C.** Team space should be configured (ideally) so that team members are facing each other with low or no barriers. 'A' is not compatible with facing each other, and 'B' is against the principles of Agile. 'D' may sound like a good idea at first glance, but the goal is not to form groups but for the team to be a single group.

73. **B.** There are only three questions asked at a daily stand-up. 1. What did you work on yesterday? 2. What are you planning to work on today? 3. What obstacles or impediments are you encountering? 'C' is the only one that fits this list.

74. **C.** Agile does not look exactly the same on all projects. That is the tradeoff of having empowered teams. 'A' would be a communications disaster, and an unnecessary one at that. 'B' is a heavy-handed approach that might create more problems that it would solve. 'D' is not a very bad answer, but this is more of a command and control approach. If teams are truly self-organizing, it means they will likely have different definitions of "done", different velocities, and different workflows. The organization should accept this and try to leverage the power of a rapidly-adapting, empowered team.

75. **C.** Planned value, also known as the Budgeted Cost of Work Scheduled, is the earned value calculation that represents the work you expect to complete at a point in time. This can be calculated on an Agile project by using team velocity to calculate the work that should be completed and the burn rate to calculate the cost of that work.

76. **B.** This describes a clear example of an information radiator.

77. **C**. This is another one straight out of The Principles Behind the Agile Manifesto. Principle six states "the most efficient and effective method of conveying information to and within a development team is face-to-face conversation." Knowing the manifesto and the principles will serve you well on the exam!

78. **C.** Toyota is the originator of asking the 5 whys in order to determine a root cause.

79. **D.** Business value is clearly the domain of the Product Owner. His or her judgment on the matter trumps everyone else's.

80. **C.** The acronym INVEST, which represents attributes of user stories, stands for (I) ndependent, (N)egotiable, (V)aluable, (E)stimable, (S)mall, and (T)estable.

81. **A.** The Agile Manifesto was written in 2001 in Snowbird, Utah.

82. **D.** Both approaches perform planning and analysis; they just do it in very different ways. 'A' is incorrect since waterfall projects do not welcome changing requirements. Instead they seek to influence the factors that cause change. 'B' is not a good answer because Agile practices short iterations, but waterfall does not. 'C' is not correct since Agile practices releases and not phases.

83. **B.** Extreme personas are exaggerated fictional characters that would use the system (often in extreme ways). This helps the team capture requirements that might otherwise be missed when focusing on typical users.

84. **D.** Iteration retrospectives are held to make future iterations more efficient. They look at the process and suggest what could be done more effectively in the future.

85. **C.** This was close, but the correct pair is that Agile projects value "Customer collaboration over contract negotiation."

86. **D.** Take note that several questions here can be answered by knowing the Principles Behind the Agile Manifesto. Principle three states that Agile projects "Deliver working software frequently, from a couple of weeks to a couple of months, with a preference to the shorter timescale." 'A' would have been a good answer if the question were about XP, but it was not an appropriate choice the way the question was worded.

87. **D.** The wording on this question is a bit tricky. Tasks are subdivisions of user stories that need to be done but do not necessarily add value. 'A' is a poor choice since capabilities (also known as epics) are very large user stories and would certainly add value. 'B' is close (this was the trap), but story points are estimates of effort, not units of work that need to be done. 'C' is a waterfall term to catch all of the people who are falling back on the PMBOK Guide here.

88. **A.** Osmotic communication describes how team members hear and absorb information just from working in the environment.

89. **B.** The team is self-organizing and self-managing, and part of that means addressing poor performance.

90. **A.** This is the very purpose of the parking lot chart. It is used to capture off-topic information that may be important but should be looked at later. 'B' is not a very good choice since it may not solve the problem at all (the stakeholder may not feel that he or she needs to refocus). 'C' is close to correct, but the way this is accomplished is through the parking lot chart, making 'A' the

better answer. 'D' isn't a good choice because we are not told what approach the team has been using, so we do not have enough information to know that changing to wireframes would have a positive impact.

91. **C.** This was an easier question. User stories are estimated in story points. 'A' is a made up term. 'B' and 'D' are among the several tools used to come up with story points, but they are not the estimate itself.

92. **B.** This was another easier question. The team is collectively responsible for the quality of the product. 'A' might have been a tempting answer, but it is not really the case. The responsibility lies with the team.

93. **C.** The WBS is a traditional, waterfall instrument, while an Agile story map is associated with Agile projects. The WBS has to be complete, meaning that it is all of the work and only the work to be done on the project. An Agile story map does not have to (and should not) be complete. It is a higher-level map than the WBS.

94. **A.** The question asked for the false statement. To answer this question you needed to remember the INVEST acronym (hopefully you are realizing this acronym is important by now). 'B', 'C', and 'D' all come directly from INVEST.

95. **D.** The key to answering this question is that they looked at the acceptance criteria and have built those into their modules first. This is what test-driven development does. It begins with the test. 'A' and 'B' are methodologies that do not prescribe that the tests have to be written first. 'C' is a practice that does incorporate testing like this, but it is not an Agile practice, and it is not mentioned in this book (which should have been a clue that it was not the right answer).

96. **B.** The definition of "done" has to be agreed upon in advance by the entire team so that they all use it in the same way. When something is marked as "done," everyone on the team needs to understand what that meant. 'A' is not necessary or even a good idea. It could be redefined, but certainly not after every iteration. 'C' is certainly not true. It needs to be the same for all deliverables. 'D' is not correct since ground rules may be unwritten and passed along more informally. The definition of done is more formal than a ground rule.

97. **A.** This is an important role question, but if you know the roles, it is not difficult. The Product Owner is primarily responsible for the product roadmap.

98. **D.** The Customer should be clear about when something "works" before it is developed. 'A' is not a good choice since delivering software that is likely not right is not a good practice. 'B' is not a good choice since it is the Customer or product owner who should do this and not the team. 'C' is not a good choice since no "test plan" is formally prescribed in Agile. This feels like a waterfall approach.

99. **C.** Planning poker should be played after the user stories have been developed and before the story points. This is because planning poker uses the user stories to create story points. 'A' is incorrect since the user stories are needed to play planning poker. 'B' is not a good choice because the story map comes before the epics, so this does not make sense. 'D' is not a good choice since the acceptance criteria should already be in place when the user stories are finished.

100. **D.** With the Wideband Delphi technique, experts giving estimates are aware of the other experts, while in traditional Delphi they do not know who the others are. This is a key difference. 'A' has it backwards. 'B' and 'C' may be true, but they may not. It is typical that both Wideband Delphi and Delphi produce a best estimate, so these are not good answers.

ANSWERS TO
PRACTICE TEST TWO

101. **B.** This should have been fairly easy. Ideal time (also called ideal days) is an estimate of time if there are no distractions or interruptions.

102. **A.** You should be prepared to see more than one question like this. Checking in new features daily is the closest reflection of continuous integration, which makes sure that updates are regularly folded back into the system to detect systemic issues quickly. 'B' is not a bad answer, but getting them into the Customer's hands is not the goal. Checking them into the system, building, and regression testing is what we're after here. 'C' is not a good answer, since unit testing is not the goal (regression testing and integration testing are). Hopefully you eliminated 'D' as a right answer quickly.

103. **A.** This should have been an easy question to answer. This is squarely the Coach's job to remind the team and help them focus on Agile principles and practices.

104. **C.** Roles are very important for this exam! The sponsor's job is to fund the project and to provide milestone-level goals for functionality and schedule. 'A' is the responsibility of the Customer or product owner. If you guessed 'B', you've probably been reading the PMBOK Guide lately. This isn't a very Agile role. 'D' is also the responsibility of the Customer or Product Owner.

105. **C.** The cycle time (the time it takes for a user story to make it through to be completed) should get shorter over time until it reaches an optimal level. 'A' is not true since iterations are fixed in duration. You may get more done in an iteration, but you should not have shorter iterations. 'B' is not a good answer, because you would hope that velocity (how many story points a team can complete in an iteration) would increase. 'D' is not a good choice, because Customer change requests is not a bad thing in Agile. In fact, once the Customer understands how easy it is to request and affect change on the product, changes are likely to increase.

106. **A.** The burn rate is amount of money the team spends during an iteration. That amount shot up during iteration 4 and 5, which could have at least two explanations: either the team worked overtime or more people were added. 'A' was the only choice that fit. 'B' is not correct, because lower efficiency would affect the velocity but not the burn rate. 'C' basically says the same thing as 'B' and is incorrect for the same reasons. 'D' is certainly not true, as burn rate does not directly tie to productivity.

107. **D.** The Team manages the iteration backlog, and the Customer or product owner manages the product backlog.

108. **C.** A burn-up chart shows story points on the Y-axis, which equates to functionality. 'D' would have been for the X-axis.

109. **A.** Agile themes are groups of stories, iterations, or releases. For example, the theme of one iteration might be "reporting," and most (or all) of the user stories might have to do with

generating reports. 'B' is a business justification. 'C' equates to a capability, and 'D' might have sounded good but it has no practical meaning.

110. **D.** The product roadmap is the document that is created after the vision statement. It has more detail than the vision statement, but it does not yet have the detail of the user stories in it. The product roadmap will show high-level features mapped to targeted releases, which is more detail than the vision statement has.

111. **A.** Product Owners are an important part of an Agile project. The term "Product Owner" is specific to Scrum, but it is similar to the Customer role in other methodologies. Because the Product Owner is so involved, he or she will be invited to many meetings, so this question was a bit difficult. Iteration retrospectives are for the core team, and they look at what was done in the preceding iteration and what could be done better in the next iteration. The team is looking at their own work, and it would not generally be productive to have a Product Owner attend this meeting. 'B' is not a good choice, since the Product Owner has a huge role to play in this meeting. 'C' is incorrect, since the Product Owner would likely attend and listen at the daily stand-up. 'D' is incorrect since the Product Owner runs the first half of the iteration planning meeting.

112. **D.** This was a tough one unless you paid attention, as any of the four potential answers could have applied. The three pillars of Scrum, as described in Chapter 9, are visibility, inspection, and adaptation.

113. **A.** Technical debt occurs when the team postpones decisions or actions that will need to be made eventually, and it is frowned upon. In this example, the team released software that presumably functioned but still needed work. This ultimately creates a backlog of work that will have to be done that will not add Customer value. 'B' is not correct since ground rules may or may not cover coding standards. 'C' should probably be true, but each team creates its own definition of done, and this may or may not be part of it. 'D' is completely wrong. Customer value is important, but not at the expense of everything else. The team still has to function within an organization, and coding standards can be an important part of that.

114. **C.** Planning poker uses a set of cards, traditionally labeled with 0, 1, 2, 3, 5, 8, 13, 20, 40, 100, and '?'. These represent story points, which are a measure of difficulty. If "ideal days" had been a choice, that would have worked also, but given the four choices presented, 'C' was the best.

115. **B.** The concept of the minimal marketable feature (MMF) is a very important one for the exam. It is the smallest unit of value to the Customer. 'A' does not work since it is an estimate and not a unit of value. 'C' was the next best guess here, but it doesn't fit as well as the MMF because of the word "set" in the question. 'D' is not a particularly Agile term, and all functions do not directly add value to the Customer.

116. **B.** Choice 'B' would have been even clearer if it stated whether it was a release retrospective or a Sprint retrospective, but it's still the best answer. 'A' is sometimes true, but not always. Not every Sprint has a subsequent release. 'C' is close as well, but the retrospective comes first. 'D' doesn't work for this. The Scrum of Scrums is for groups of Scrum teams to get together and discuss what has been accomplished since the last meeting. They are often held daily.

117. **D.** The information radiator is a great resource for current information. It may be inadequate for the stakeholder's particular needs, but it is a great place to start. 'A' is not really the job of the coach. While the coach may be asked to give statuses, he or she won't gather them at daily stand-ups as this answer suggests. 'B' is not a good answer. This is not the Product Owner's job. 'C' is not a great answer since it is not productive for the team to stop working and give a status every time a stakeholder requests one.

118. **A.** This is slightly tricky. Iteration H is also known as a hardening iteration, where no new functionality is developed but the functionality that is there is tested.

119. **C.** The Scrum of Scrum meetings allows for the various teams to meet and coordinate their work. This would be ideal (and probably necessary) on a Scrum program.

120. **B.** The Product Owner is the single voice of the Customer and users on the project.

121. **C.** This one was not easy. Iterations are commitments by the team to accomplish a set package of work, and once an iteration is begun, it is important to try to protect it so that the team can meet that commitment. The Customer can always add functionality to the product backlog, but the iteration backlog should be static once the iteration has begun. 'A' was a trick answer. Welcoming change is a good thing, but not when it involves changing an iteration in the middle of that iteration. 'B' is not a good answer, since the team has interests here as well. 'D' is the worst of the four answers. The ScrumMaster or coach does not have the final say about this (or much else) on the project.

122. **A.** There are 12 XP practices, and if the team cannot apply all 12, it is recommended that they start with the first 6.

123. **C.** The product backlog needs to be groomed, and it is the Product Owner or Customer's job to do this.

124. **A.** Risks are any uncertainty and may be positive or negative, so there are risks that projects could finish early just like there are risks they could finish late. In this case, the team is performing better than planned since they are burning down story points faster than the linear plan, so there is a risk they will finish early. 'B' is the opposite of what this chart shows. There is no reason in this scenario to choose 'C' since we have no data showing that they risk going over budget. 'D' might look tempting, but consider that the team could have added more people to achieve this result, which might put them over budget. The fact is, we can't tell that from the chart.

125. **D.** Epic stories are large stories that have not been broken down, and these are typically found at or near the bottom of the product backlog. As they are moved up closer to the top, they will need to be broken down further.

126. **C.** This might have been a tricky question for you. Sprints are not ceremonies. They are where the core of work takes place, but ceremonies are akin to meetings, and the Sprint does not qualify. 'A', 'B', and 'D' all are.

127. **A.** Agile and traditional projects differ in many ways. One of them is that Agile projects favor being able to adapt to the environment and to change, while traditional projects like to anticipate requirements and change in advance. 'B' is not a good choice, since both use the plan-do-check-act cycle (although they use it differently). 'C' is not the best choice since Agile is very process-oriented, and it's not accurate to say it favors the product. 'D' is not a good choice since traditional methods do not necessarily favor the organization. They may favor team as much as an Agile project does.

128. **D.** In a product backlog, the items at the top should be clear, while the ones at the bottom will likely be less defined. Large, aggregated epic stories will likely be at the bottom of the product backlog and will be disaggregated as they progress upward.

129. **D.** Yes, it is a problem. This is the Product Owner's show where he or she uses the first half of this meeting explaining the user stories to the team from a functionality standpoint.

130. **B.** The most important pending user story should be prioritized at the top of the product backlog.

131. **B.** Agile projects still plan, and some practitioners claim they plan more than traditional projects. They simply do the planning closer to the actual work. 'A' was a trap that misrepresented the Agile Manifesto. The correct pairs are that Agile follows customer collaboration over contract negotiation and responding to change over following a plan. 'C' is not generally accurate, and 'D' is completely wrong. Planning is important for Agile projects.

132. **D.** A spike solution is a rapid experiment to answer a question rather than endlessly debate it. This looks like an ideal scenario for one.

133. **A.** Product Owners are not encouraged to tinker with an iteration once it has started. It represents a commitment by the team to deliver a certain amount of work, and it should be respected by everyone.

134. **B.** The Customer or Product Owner is responsible for writing the user stories.

135. **A.** 15 minutes is the rule for daily stand-ups. They are often held standing up to encourage the team to keep it short.

136. **D.** The release plan is not set in stone. It is a fluid document that may be adjusted, depending on team velocity and priorities. 'A' is true of an iteration but not of a release plan. 'B' is reversed. A single release may contain multiple iterations but not the other way around. 'C' is not true. The Coach or SrumMaster does not drive the release plan. The Customer or Product Owner does.

137. **C.** Decide as late as possible is the 3rd principle of Lean.

138. **C.** Costs may be estimated primarily as a function of the team's burn rate and velocity, but they may also factor in the backlog and release plan. 'A' is incorrect, since this is too early. The product backlog can contain epic stories that may not be easily estimated. 'B' is not a good choice since the team is generally expected to be the same size and to maintain a consistent burn rate from one iteration to the next, and the lengths of iterations are fixed. Even if they become more efficient, the costs won't drop since the same number of people are working the same number of days. 'D' is not accurate, since costs often have to be calculated before an iteration and not just after one.

139. **A.** The question is somewhat vague, but the point is important. The Coach or ScrumMaster should appreciate some conflict. Too much conflict or conflict with too much intensity may be problematic, but some conflict is a sign of a healthy team. If a team is trying too hard to preserve harmony then it could be doing so at the expense of more important items.

140. **B.** This is an important point. Agile projects can be difficult to compare, but there has to be a basis for comparison. The return on investment between two teams makes the most sense in the scenarios presented (even though this one has its difficulties). 'A' is not a good choice. Velocities are based on story points, and story points are going to differ between teams. For instance, two teams might value the same user story at 10 story points and 100 story points, which could translate into roughly the same effort. 'C' presents an interesting comparison by looking at cycle time, but if one team has a faster cycle time than another but costs 4 times as much, is it better? It is impossible to give a blanket answer to that. 'D' doesn't work for the same reasons that answer 'A' doesn't work. 'B' is the best choice, since ROI is a more objective measure that can be applied across projects.

141. **A.** An Agile schedule may be built by estimating story points, prioritizing, and dividing by velocity. 'B' and 'C' are approaches from the classic waterfall method. 'D' could be true in some cases, but it is certainly not the rule, and while timeboxing sets the time for deliverables, it may not give as much detail as a schedule would.

142. **D.** The information radiator is posted in a highly visible location, and it is communicates information to the stakeholders and to the team. When this is done properly, information is

transparent and easily accessible. 'A is not a good choice since the project management plan probably does not exist in a meaningful format on a truly Agile project, and if it does, it would not suffice as the primary means of communication. 'B' is the classic waterfall answer and does not apply here. 'C' was a good choice, but the team should not be tied up in face-to-face meetings.

143. **D.** Timeboxing does constrain the team, although it is not in a particularly negative way. It simply prescribes that the schedule is not flexible, but the scope is. 'A' was incorrect since neither the iterations nor the releases are particularly flexible with schedule in this scenario. 'B' is incorrect since the planning time is not affected by timeboxing. 'C' may sound correct at first, but only the deliverable date is set and not the overall schedule. The team still has the freedom to work that out.

144. **A.** The Team meets daily for the 15-minute daily stand-up.

145. **B.** The Product Owner is primarily responsible for the product backlog. 'A', 'C', and 'D' are all responsibilities of the team.

146. **D.** Even though the Customer has a legitimate issue, the Daily stand-up meetings have a different purpose. In this case, it is the ScrumMaster's job to help keep the team focused on Agile. If you guessed 'A', be aware that "team" is not always the right answer. Know the roles well. 'B' is not a good answer since we have no reason to escalate this to the sponsor. The team probably should do 'C' but not in the daily stand-up. It has a different purpose.

147. **A.** Agile works best in projects that are complex and where the requirements are mostly undetermined.

148. **C.** Because it has been sorted by risk and not only by value, the risk-adjusted backlog will be in a different order. 'A' or 'B' could potentially be true, but it depends on the approach to risk. 'D' is not a good choice since the backlog only shows undeveloped (future) user stories, and so the potential risk events would only be looking into the future.

149. **A.** Lean has several core principles, including 'B', 'C', and 'D'. Test as early as possible sounds like a great idea, but it is not explicitly a core part of Lean.

150. **C.** Risks do not have to be quantified to be understood. They may be qualitatively analyzed instead. 'A' is an accurate definition of risk. 'B' is an accurate way to represent risk, and 'D' is absolutely correct. Value and risk are tied together and must be evaluated in light of each other.

151. **D.** The active listening model includes listening, understanding, retaining, and actively responding. It does not include recording.

152. **C.** The most likely reason for an Agile team to play innovation games would be to help gather requirements.

153. **B.** Agile teams are self-managing.

154. **A.** The planning game is an XP practice for writing user stories and estimating them. The stated goal of the planning game is to maximize value.

155. **C.** Personas are fictitious identities created to look at how users might use the product.

156. **B.** Engineering tasks are generally created during iteration planning when the Team breaks down user stories in to specific development tasks. 'A' is not a good choice, since the Product Owner likely writes user stories without direct involvement of the Team, but it is the Team that defines tasks.

157. **D.** It is the Product Owner's primarily responsibility to ensure that the product meets its ROI.

158. **B.** Technical debt occurs when the Team postpones a necessary technical decision.

159. **C.** The term DRY is an Agile acronym for "Don't Repeat Yourself."

160. **C.** While it could have been represented in one of several ways, ideal days was the best choice here. 'A' is not accurate since tasks are not estimates. 'B' is the amount of time it takes a user story to go from a specification to functioning software. 'D' is the number of user stories that a Team can deliver in a period of time.

161. **D.** The empowered Team is responsible for managing the iteration backlog (the Product Owner manages the product backlog).

162. **A.** Systems Development Life Cycle (SDLC) is practically synonymous with the waterfall approach. 'B' has little to do with Agile or waterfall. 'C' was the trap here. Agile is a form of project management just like waterfall is. 'D' is inaccurate, since Agile projects also use Deming's cycle. They just use it in smaller iterations than most waterfall projects do.

163. **C.** Metaphor is the 3rd principle of eXtreme Programming (XP).

164. **B.** Agile tooling is any software or artifact that helps the team focus on Agile principles and builds a sense of team. Version control software fits this definition.

165. **A.** If you struggled with this, look at the question again. The word "Coach" should clue you in that we are talking about eXtreme Programming, and the Coach's job is to help the team follow the Agile process, reflected in the 12 XP principles. 'B' and 'C' are great pursuits, but they are not the Coach's main focus. 'D' is not a good choice at all. It represents the top-down command and control style that is not compatible with Agile.

166. **D.** For the payback period, a smaller number is more desirable. 'A' does not really make sense in this context. 'B' is not good, since many organizations use this as a primary means of making decisions – especially if they do not want their cash tied up for a long period of time. 'C' is almost correct, but payback period could rationally be compared with other projects outside of the organization.

167. **C.** Burn-down charts show features on the vertical (Y) axis, which translate to scope and time on the horizontal (X) axis, which translates to schedule, making 'C' the best choice. 'A' does not work, since you cannot calculate cycle time (the time it takes to go from specification to working software) from a burn-down chart. 'B' would have been the next best guess since burn-down charts certainly can be used in risk management, but few would consider them to be a primary tool. 'D' is not a good choice since cost is not represented on a burn-down chart, and without more data there is no way to calculate it.

168. **A.** Ideal time is time with no interruptions or distractions. None of the other choices really matter, but interruptions does take away from ideal time.

169. **A.** This should have been easy. It is the definition of the team's velocity.

170. **B.** The Product Owner takes on most of the risk for the product. The other roles take on risk for the project to varying degrees, but the Product Owner is defining value and is responsible for stating what the customer wants.

171. **D.** This is a different twist on another question in this final. An Agile project's schedule may be established, in part, by dividing story points by the velocity. 'A', 'B', and 'C' are more related to waterfall project management.

172. **B.** This ties back to the usage of the terms "chickens" and "pigs" (see the glossary if you're confused). 'A' does not work well since the stakeholder should be allowed to come and listen to the meeting but should certainly not participate. 'C' is not a good choice at all. The Sprint retrospective is for the team and not for outsiders. 'D' is a waste of time for the Team.

173. **C.** The most logical explanation is that stories were added to the backlog, causing the line to spike. 'A' is not a good choice since the cycle time is not reflected on a burn-down chart. 'B' is not accurate since velocity represents the team's speed and not the number of user stories. 'D' is incorrect since neither the number of team members nor their cost is reflected on the release burn-down chart.

174. **B.** This question is a bit difficult. 'B' is the best overall answer given the information at hand. The key to answering it is to think about maximizing Customer value. Since the velocity (the number of story points a team can deliver in one iteration) is fixed at 16, the assumption is that the team cannot exceed this threshold in an iteration. That means that the priorities have to be shuffled to get as much value as possible into each iteration. While it would be far preferable to involve the Product Owner or Customer in this, that is not an option we are given in the scenario. Therefore, 'B' delivers the most value to the Customer.

175. **B.** This should have been an easy one for you. "Done" is agreed upon by the entire team.

176. **A.** Kanban is a Japanese management term that, literally translated, means "signal." 'B' is the translation for another Japanese management term, "Kaizen."

177. **B.** Since the iteration has ended, the feature should be added to the next iteration backlog. 'A' is not a good choice, since we aren't looking for a "quick fix" and the iteration is over. 'C' is the worst place to bring this up. 'D' might be a good idea, but we don't know that we are practicing test-first development here, nor do we know if that had anything to do with the customer's refusal to accept the feature.

178. **A.** Agile projects practice daily stand-up meetings. The primary purpose of these meetings is to coordinate the team's efforts.

179. **D.** All things being equal, the team's velocity should be improving over time. While there are many things that could affect this, it would be a concern.

180. **D.** Kanban boards do not help visualize the backlog. They only show work-in-progress (WIP). 'A' is a function of a Kanban board. They show WIP and are used to encourage the team to limit the amount of work they are performing at any given point in time. 'B' is correct, since the Kanban board may be a key part of the overall information radiator. C' is exactly what Kanban boards do by showing how items progress through different stages.

181. **D.** The charter is not optional for Agile projects, making it the most important one up here. 'A', 'B', and 'C' are all more closely associated with traditional projects, and you would not necessarily expect to find them on an Agile project.

182. **B.** The best choice of the four is to try to create a live presence through technology. 'A' is impractical. You cannot simply insist that everyone be brought together physically. Virtual teams are very much a reality. 'C' is not going to fly on an Agile exam. 'D' is naïve. You certainly do need to adapt to this situation.

183. **C.** The product vision statement is an important document that states what the product is, why it is needed, and why someone would pay for it. It does not describe why Agile is the right approach.

184. **A.** The product roadmap describes what releases are planned and what relevant features they would have.

185. **D.** The product backlog should be DEEP, standing for (D)etailed Appropriately, (E)stimable, (E)mergent, and (P)rioritized.

186. **C.** This was a more difficult question. It required you to know how Wideband Delphi is used. In this technique the range is plotted on a graph to be used for discussion.

187. **B.** Affinity estimating is designed to be fast and to rapidly move through a large backlog. 'A' and 'C' may be relatively quick, but they are not as fast as affinity estimating.

188. **A.** Leas' conflict model describes 5 levels of conflict: (1) A problem to solve, (2) Disagreement, (3) Contest, (4) Fight or Flight, (5) World War.

189. **A.** Unfortunately EVM is not generally as accurate on Agile projects since the scope of work (and thus the planned value) is not clearly defined. 'B' is not the case. In fact, given Agile's simpler calculations for velocity and linear nature of story points, it is actually easier to calculate. 'C' is close, but the cone of uncertainty doesn't particularly impact EVM. 'D' may sound good, but it is very different on Agile since Agile does not plan everything out in advance.

190. **B.** This is a classic example of a Cumulative Flow Diagram (CFD). It shows items that are moving through the system as well as those that have not been started and those that are complete. A Kanban board would have also fit the description in the question, but it was not one of the 4 choices.

191. **C.** Lean is based on the seven principles of Eliminate Waste, Amplify Learning, Decide as Late as Possible, Deliver as Fast as Possible, Empower the Team, Build Integrity In, and See the Whole.

192. **B.** Agile methodologies work best in environments that require complex decision making. 'A' is not a good choice for Agile, since roles and goals will be difficult to define. 'C' does not work well since environments where things are relatively close to agreement and certainty might do better with waterfall. 'D' means basically the same thing as 'A'.

193. **D.** You would have gotten this one from reading the glossary. An information refrigerator is a chart or artifact that has to be opened and unpacked to be understood. It is not meant to be transparent. 'A', 'B', and 'C' are not Agile terms nor are they found in the glossary (hint, hint).

194. **B.** The product backlog represents the work remaining on the project. 'A' is not accurate since the iteration backlog only shows the work remaining for this iteration. 'C' and 'D' may be useful artifacts, but they do not show work remaining on the project.

195. **D.** Agile embraces uncertainty, but waterfall tries to manage it by removing it.

196. **C.** The iteration burn-down chart is an excellent resource for showing how the current iteration is progressing. 'A' and 'B' could certainly answer the question, but the iteration burn-down chart was designed to show this. 'D' is not a good choice since the release plan does not show information about the current iteration.

197. **A.** While none of the four answers was particularly complete, Agile teams need individuals who are generalists and can maintain everyone else's code. 'B' represents siloing and is not a good choice. 'C' would be good on a waterfall project, but Agile projects are more about the team than self-direction. 'D' is not a good choice since conflict avoidance is not favored within project management.

198. **D.** Iteration reviews are all about the team demonstrating the features for the customer. 'A' is not a good choice since the team meets to talk about how to do things better in the next iteration. 'B' is a chance for different teams to meet and coordinate their efforts. 'C' is a made-up term more appropriate for movie stars than Agile practitioners.

199. **A.** Remember that user stories are negotiable, meaning that the developer and customer sometimes need to work them out together. There is nothing wrong with a customer to ask to speak with the developer about a user story or a piece of functionality. In this case, the iteration backlog would show who was working on the component in question. 'B' would not show it since components are assigned at the iteration level and not at the release level. 'C' was the trap here. While the team is responsible for the results, they will not all be working on the component. 'D' would not be an efficient way to find this information out when all the customer really needs to do is to look at the iteration backlog.

200. **B.** The risk-adjusted backlog is a primary way in which risk is managed. 'A' and 'C' are not good choices since they represent more of a waterfall approach. 'D' is a technique used to evaluate risk, but it is not the primary way it is managed on an Agile project, leaving 'B' as the best overall answer here.

INDEX

INDEX

INDEX

F

G

H

I

K

L

THE PMI-ACP EXAM

INDEX